CLUEDLE

ROCKET
FOX

50
FIENDISHLY
FUN FAST
PUZZLES

CLUEDLE

5
MINUTE
MYSTERY
PUZZLES
Round the World

HARTIGAN BROWNE

Published 2026 by Rocket Fox,
an imprint of Pan Macmillan
The Smithson, 6 Briset Street, London EC1M 5NR
EU representative: Macmillan Publishers Ireland Ltd, 1st Floor,
The Liffey Trust Centre, 117–126 Sheriff Street Upper, Dublin 1 D01 YC43
Associated companies throughout the world

ISBN 978-1-0350-8957-4

1 3 5 7 9 8 6 4 2

A CIP catalogue record for this book is available from the British Library.

Printed and bound in the UK using 100% Renewable Electricity by CPI Group (UK) Ltd

Visit **www.panmacmillan.com** to read more about all our books and to buy them.

Aloha, young detective!

World-famous detective Hartigan Browne here, in search of an agent in possession of razor-sharp wit and an adventurous spirit. If this sounds like you, read on!

With dastardly crimes occurring across the globe, the Hartigan Browne Detective Agency has decided to go global and take on cases in continents other than our own. Will you help?

As you trot the globe, you'll tackle fifty teasing tasks that should take five minutes or under to solve. But don't expect it all to be a cruise . . . beyond the buzzing cities and paradise islands, a whole host of baddies with criminal intentions awaits.

If you think you have what it takes, quickly pack a suitcase and grab your passport. It's time to embark on an epic adventure as an international crime fighter.

Bon voyage!

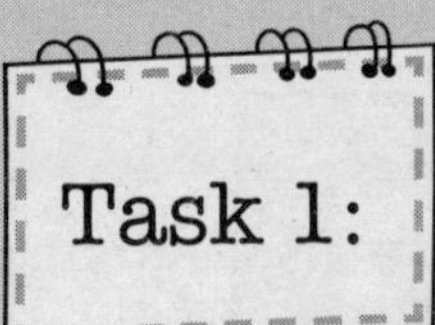

Task 1: What Am I?

Hey diddle-diddle, here are three riddles, before I bid you farewell.

If you're scratching your head, let it never be said that I don't test your little grey cells!

HARTIGAN'S HINT:
Mail, dock, tracks.

2. When you need me, you throw me away. When you've finished with me, you take me back. What am I?

— — — — — — — —

3. The more you take, the more you leave behind. What am I?

— — — — — — — — —

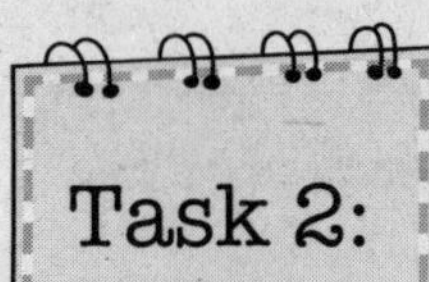

Task 2: Prepare for Take-off

Suspects fly in and out of airports each and every day. Let's test your observation skills by finding the following airport-related words. The words may be hiding forwards, backwards, up, down or diagonally.

ARRIVALS	DEPARTURES
BAGGAGE	GATE
BUS	PLANE
CABIN	RESTAURANT
CAROUSEL	RUNWAY
COCKPIT	SHOP
CREW	TERMINAL
CUSTOMS	TRAVELATOR

Then rearrange the shaded letters to reveal one person to keep under surveillance, and fill in the answer below the grid. Watch out, your suspect may be hiding in *plain* sight!

V	B	N	Q	W	K	D	C	U	S	T	O	M	S
I	C	C	I	S	H	E	O	V	A	D	X	L	R
H	O	D	J	A	T	P	L	O	S	J	E	H	U
Y	C	T	X	L	R	A	D	Q	C	I	Y	D	N
W	K	B	Y	N	Z	R	H	K	N	R	B	F	W
J	P	S	K	C	B	T	I	F	Z	I	E	T	A
L	I	S	Q	A	D	U	N	V	U	T	K	W	Y
E	T	H	F	O	O	R	L	E	A	O	R	M	Q
S	E	O	D	H	E	E	Y	G	N	L	E	J	V
U	I	P	X	U	V	S	K	A	O	W	S	K	E
O	B	N	L	D	M	R	J	G	M	Y	T	Z	C
R	F	S	A	A	Q	C	P	G	X	D	A	S	T
A	H	K	N	A	N	M	L	A	R	K	U	B	O
C	A	B	I	N	W	E	Y	B	A	B	R	F	S
O	V	E	M	R	B	F	O	H	T	C	A	D	W
B	D	J	R	S	Z	U	X	D	K	Q	N	V	L
X	Y	O	E	C	T	Q	N	J	I	K	T	H	X
C	H	L	T	R	A	V	E	L	A	T	O	R	F

Suspect: _ _ _ _ _

Answer on page 104

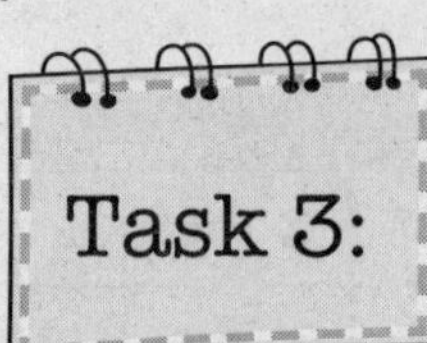

Task 3: Agents Abroad

I only entrust the very best HBDA agents to complete missions beyond our borders. Let's see how you stack up, shall we?

Fill in the missing vowels to discover the qualities that each of my agents must possess. The first one has been written for you.

1. P<u>U</u>NCT<u>U</u> <u>A</u>L<u>I</u>TY

2. S__NS__ __F __DV__NT__R__

3. S__ __ L __GS

4. H__ __ D F__ R H__ __GHTS

5. C__R__ __S__TY

6. L__NG__ __G__ SK__LLS

7. PHYS__ C__L F__TN__SS

8. S__NS__ __F D__R__CT__ __N

That's some top-notch deduction, detective! Now tick the boxes above next to the assets you believe apply to you.

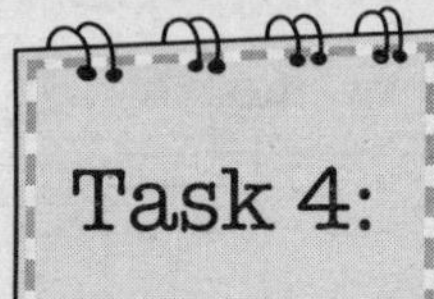

Task 4: Taking Flight

You arrive at the airport to embark on an overseas investigation with your destination still to be confirmed. To work out where you're being sent, solve this next teaser using the helpful clues.

- The plane is not delayed.
- The gate is an even number.
- The flight number contains a vowel.
- The plane is due to depart before two o'clock in the afternoon.

Time	Destination	Flight	Gate	Remarks
13.18	AMSTERDAM	LH177	02	FINAL CALL
13.20	HONG KONG	JU626	11	DELAYED
13.25	MONTREAL	AC228	04	DELAYED
13.39	CAPE TOWN	SG190	13	ON TIME
13.45	SEOUL	TO888	07	BOARDING
13.48	ZANZIBAR	ZA302	06	BOARDING
14.00	NEW YORK	OP456	12	CLOSING
14.05	MADRID	QA101	08	DELAYED
14.30	DUBLIN	DB020	10	ON TIME
14.55	MUNICH	GM460	18	ON TIME

Write the name of your destination here:

____

Super sleuthing, detective. Now what are you waiting for? Head straight to your gate!

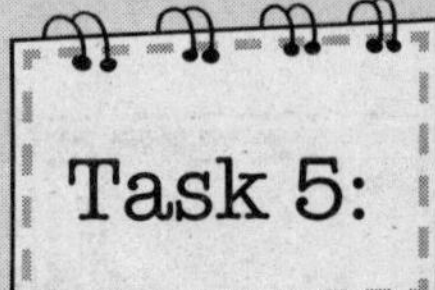

Task 5: Onwards and Upwards

I hope you have a head for heights, young agent. This next task requires you to climb two ladders to snoop on a suspect.

Start at the bottom of the ladders, then change one letter on each rung, using the clues, to form a new word.

Puzzle A:

The opposite of warm.

A thin string or rope.

Something you might send on a birthday.

A room in a hospital.

START

HARTIGAN'S HINT:
R changes to an **S** in the below example.
The opposite of slow. FA**S**T
START: FA**R**T

W A R M

Puzzle B:

'Suit' or 'brief' could go before this word.

The actors in a film or show.

The opposite of future.

An agreement or promise.

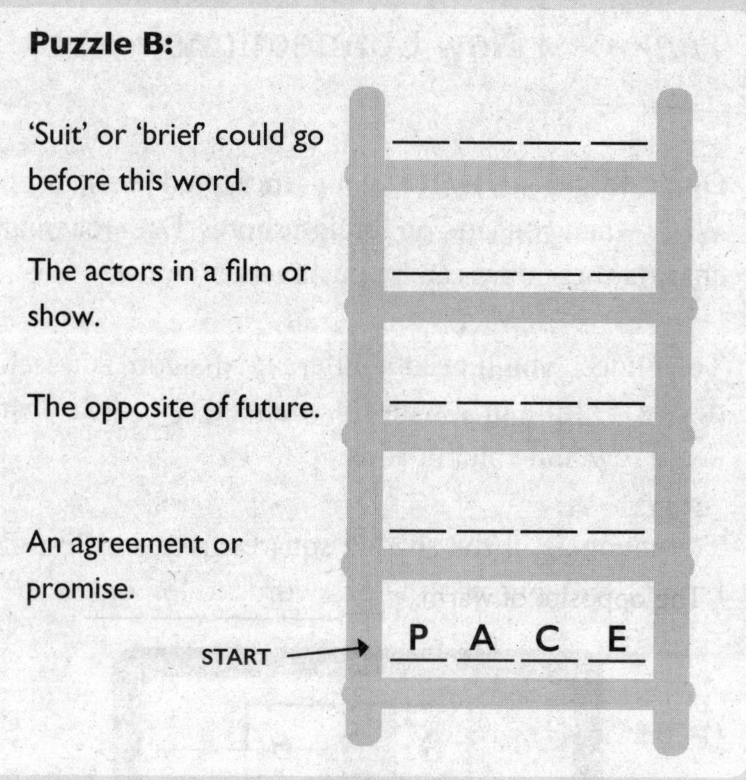

Now combine your answers at the top of each ladder to reveal another expression for an unsolved crime:

___ ___ ___ ___   ___ ___ ___ ___

Bravo detective, you've gone up in my estimation already!

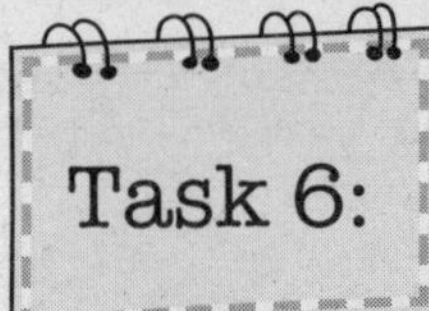

New Connections

Don't forget to switch your encrypted devices to Wi-Fi when you land on foreign shores. Data roaming charges these days can be positively criminal!

To connect, you'll need a different password for each device. Fill the grid with the numbers 1 to 9 so that every row and column adds up to 15.

The numbers in the shaded squares from smallest to biggest will give you the passwords to log on.

A.

Password:

B.

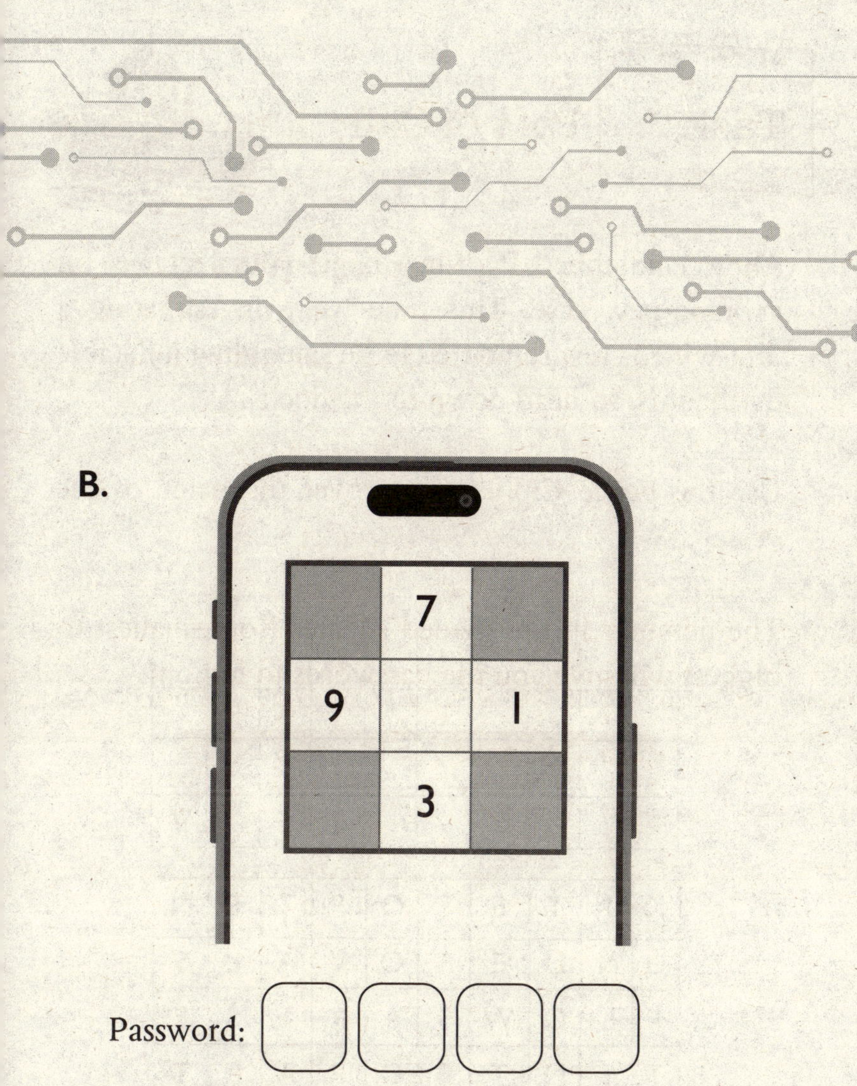

Password:

Super sleuthing, detective. You're up and running!

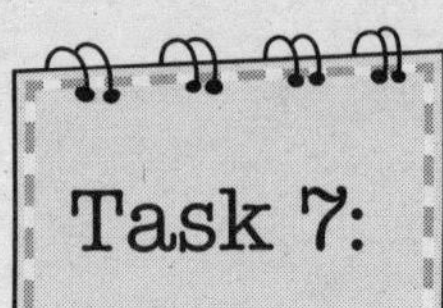

Task 7: Port of Call

Ahoy, landlubber! It's time to get your feet wet on a brand-new case. This time we're investigating a dim-witted crew rumoured to be smuggling inflatable dartboards, so head down to the docks.

Use the Fence Cipher to uncover the name of the vessel . . .

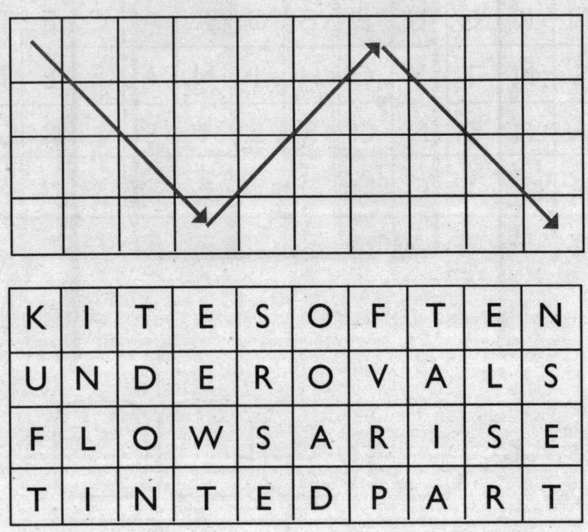

Answer here: __ __ __ __   __ __   __ __ __ __

HARTIGAN'S HINT:
Follow the arrows from left to right.

Now work out when and where it's due to dock . . .

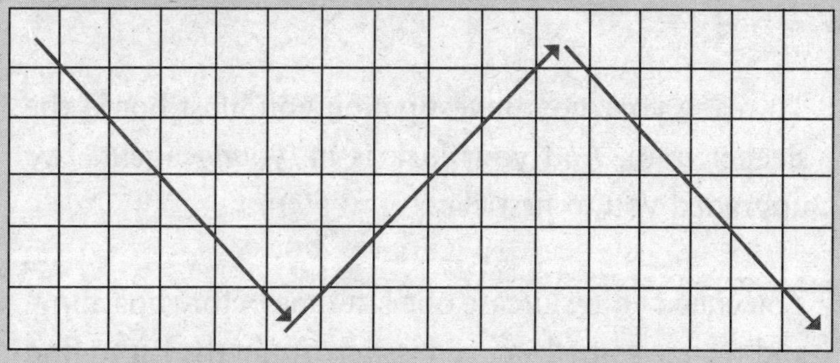

Answer here:

_ _ _ _ _ _ _ , _ _ _ _ _ _ _ _ _

Well, blow me down! You sailed through that test.
Now navigate to where the ship is due to ap-pier.

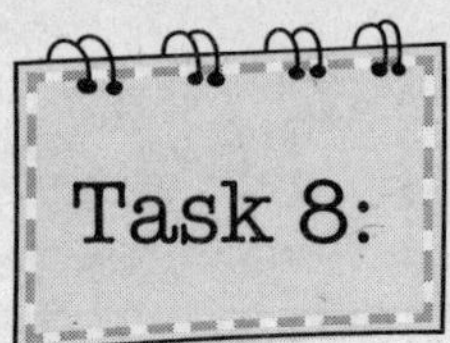

Snoozing in Style

To reach your next investigation you must board the sleeper train. And your luck is in, young agent. I've upgraded you to first class!

You check your suitcase one last time before boarding, and realize something is missing. Study the list to find the missing travel essential. Circle one letter from each item and work down the list in order. The first and last letters have been done for you.

Notes:

- ✓ LAPTOP
- ✓ T-SHIRT
- ✓ SOCKS
- ✓ NOTEBOOK
- ✓ HEADPHONES
- ✓ TOOTHBRUSH

Write your answer here:

T _ _ _ _ T

HARTIGAN'S HINT: Travelling without
this item may prove a costly mistake.

The shores of a Scottish loch are the destination for this evening's mission. Another of my staff, Agent Pattie Lightfoot, has promised a clue will present itself when you least expect it.

You look down at the lapping waves and, lo and behold, there it is! A bottle glinting in the moonlight! You pick it up, unscrew the cap and discover a note you're sure is from Lightfoot – she sent you the key to the cipher earlier. Use the key to decipher Lightfoot's note.

Key:

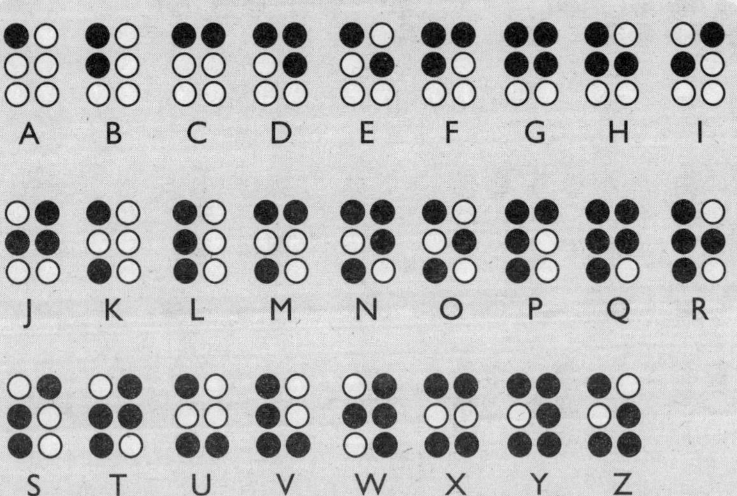

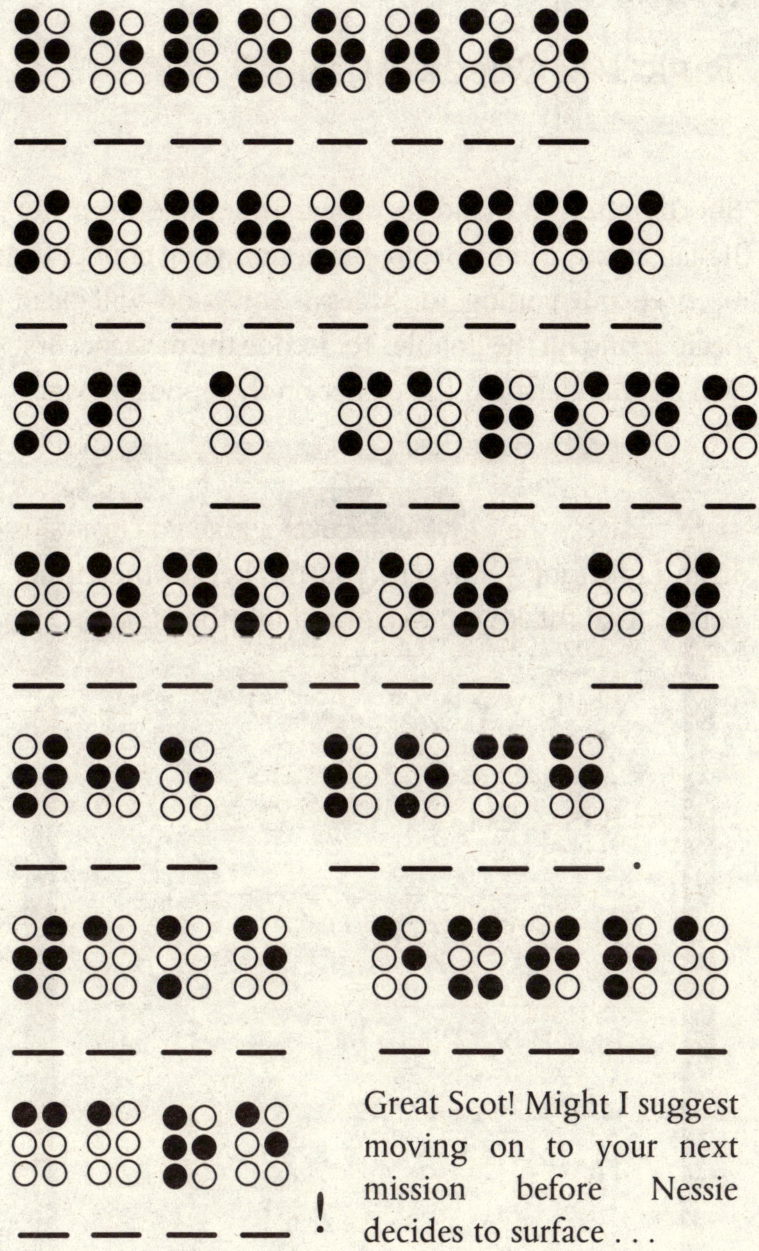

Great Scot! Might I suggest moving on to your next mission before Nessie decides to surface . . .

Task 10: Checking In

Shortly after you land in Rome, a message from our Italian agent, Monti Baldo, buzzes on your phone. It's been encoded using the Caesar Shift and will need deciphering on the double. To decode the message, first you must understand the cipher on the opposite page.

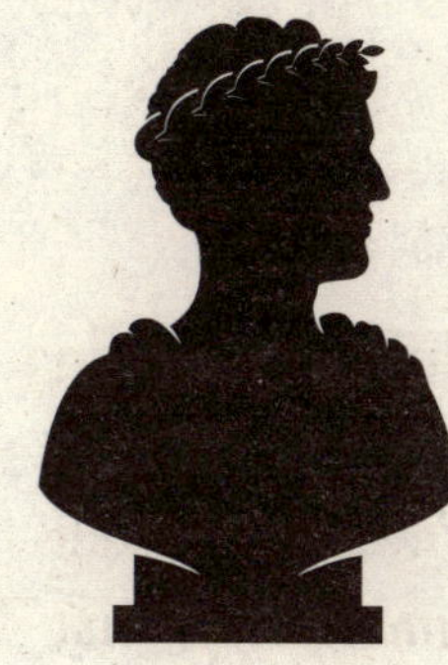

This ancient cipher is named after Julius Caesar, who used it to keep the contents of his private letters under wraps. Complete the rest of the cipher, counting the same number shift each time.

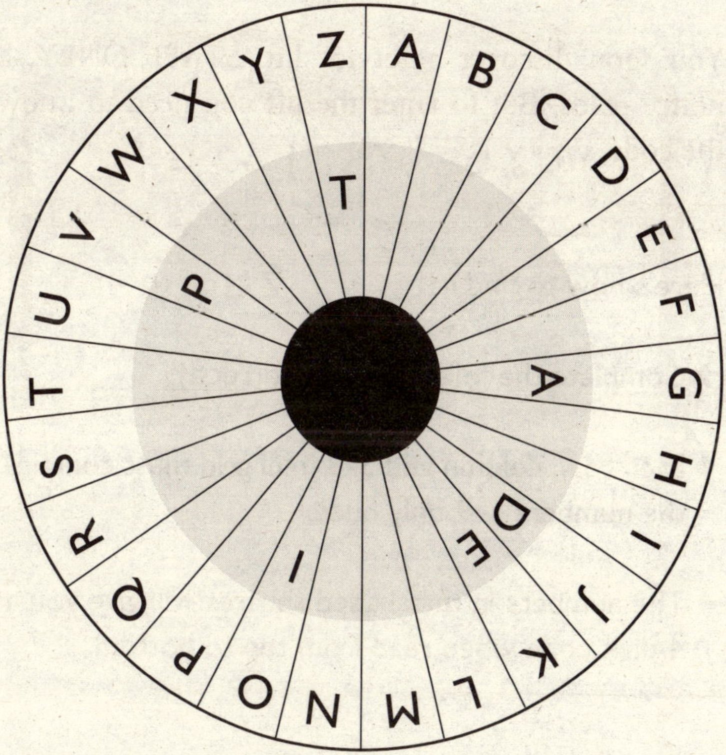

Answer on page 107

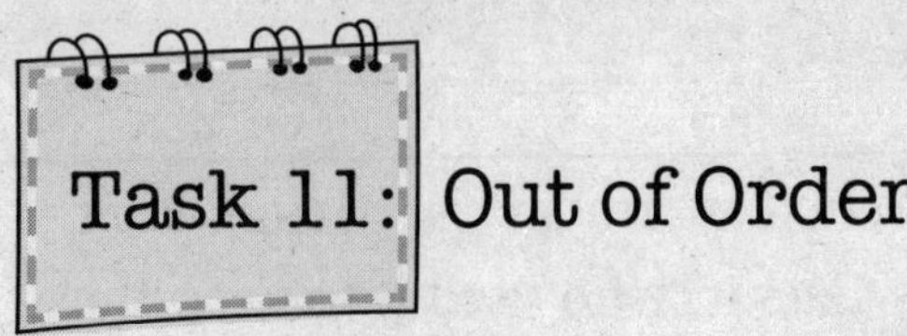

On your latest jaunt to investigate a dubious case in Dubai, you are given a key to your hotel room on the twenty-fifth floor. *Room with a view? Delightful!* you tell yourself. What the receptionist fails to mention is that the lift is out of order!

You soon discover a service lift. STAFF ONLY, a notice reads. But to enter the lift you need to know the code.

Here's how to find it:

⟶ Complete the following grid correctly.

⟶ Each row, column and 3x3 mini grid must contain the numbers 1–9 only once.

⟶ The numbers in the shaded squares will give you a 4-digit code when read from top to bottom.

Now punch in the code and head on up!

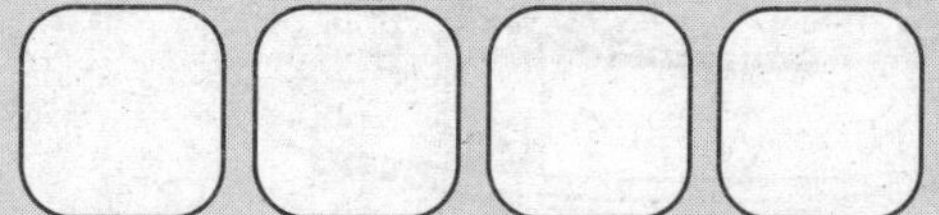

Task 12: Grounded

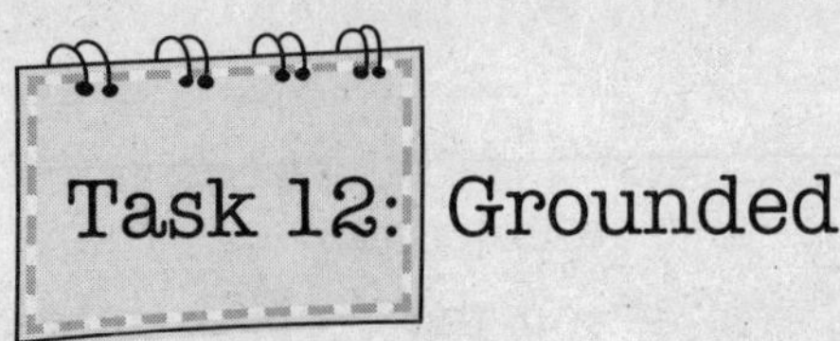

You board the Centennial Wheel in the pod ahead of a suspect believed to be travelling using a fake passport. 'Eileen Dover' sounds entirely fictional!

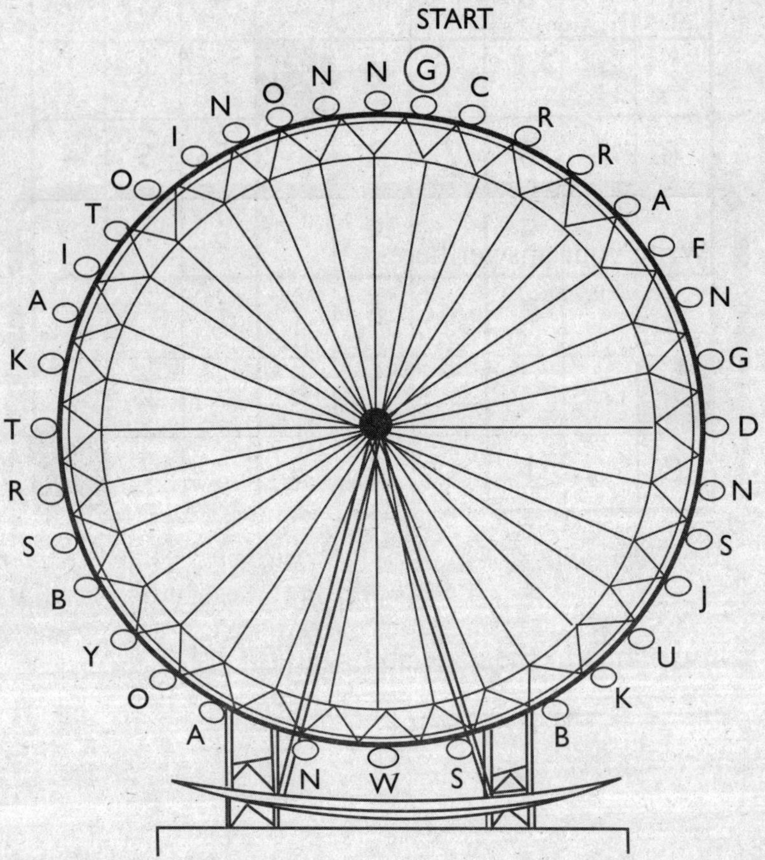

But when it's Ms Dover's turn to enter the ride, the suspect decides to keep her feet on the ground and flees the scene. Rats!

Fortuitously, our Chicagoan counterpart, Agent Windy Winberg, has also been keeping one eye on the wheel. Circle every second letter to confirm the latest sighting of this preposterous phoney.

Write your answer here:

__ __ __ __ __   __ __ __ __ __ __

__ __ __ __ __ __ __ __

Task 13: Missed Call

Upon landing at London's Heathrow Airport, you switch off 'airplane mode' on your phone and discover a voicemail that our very own Agent Lightfoot left you earlier.

When you play it back, all you can hear is a series of beeps – some long and some short. Curious! Then you realize . . . the message had been encrypted using Morse code. Use the Morse code alphabet key to help you translate her message.

A	.–	J	.– – –	S	...
B	–...	K	–.–	T	–
C	–.–.	L	.–..	U	..–
D	–..	M	– –	V	...–
E	.	N	–.	W	.– –
F	..–.	O	– – –	X	–..–
G	– –.	P	.– –.	Y	–.– –
H	....	Q	– –.–	Z	– –..
I	..	R	.–.		

—·· · ·— —··

—·· ·—· ——— ·—

··· — · ·—— ··· / ——— ··—·

··· ——— ·· — ····

— ——— ·— · ·—·

— —·— ·—— · ·—·

—··· ·—· ·· —·· — ·

HARTIGAN'S HINT: London's calling! Pick up!

Answer on page 108

27

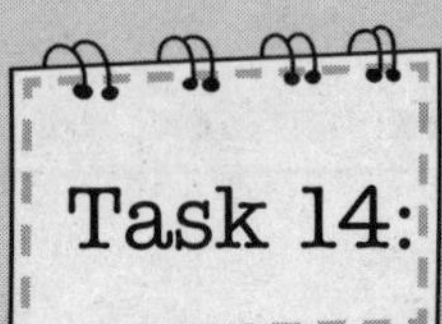

Task 14: Take the Wheel

It's impossible to become a world-famous detective without first travelling the world, and I should know . . . I've cracked poisoning cases in Papua New Guinea and foiled frauds in the frozen Arctic.

Now it's over to you. Hidden in these word wheels are four-wheeled vehicles that will help you navigate the globe. You must use all the letters only once.

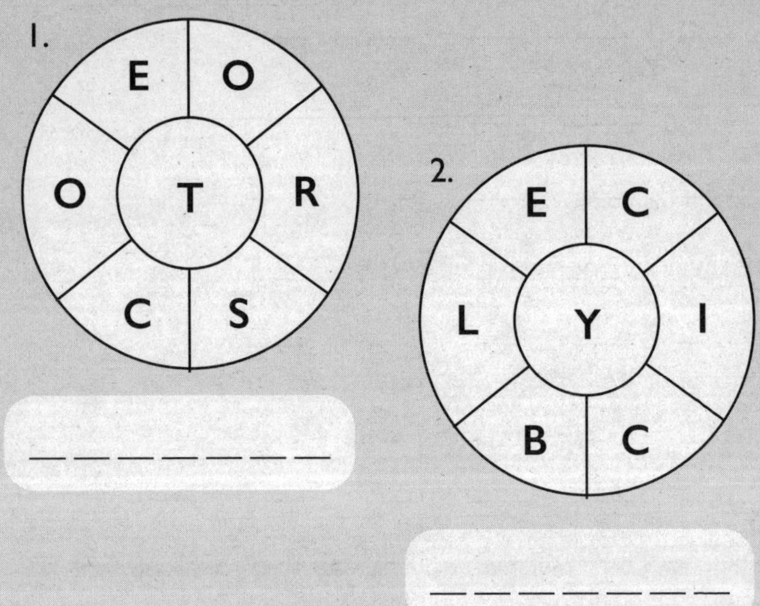

Now try nine letters.

3.

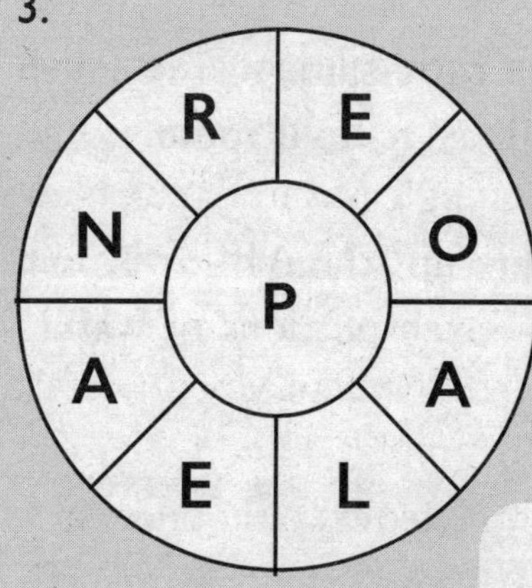

4.

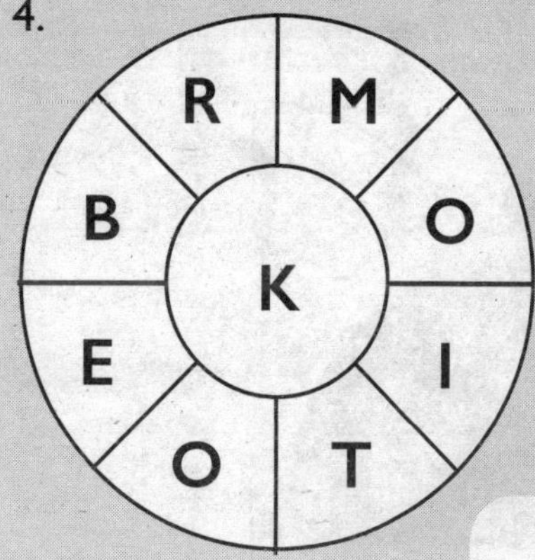

Answer on page 109

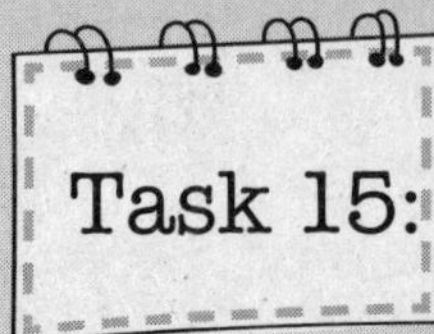

Task 15: Breakfast in Bed

Today's mission requires an early start, so I've taken the liberty of ordering breakfast to your room.

It seems there's been a mix-up, though, as Room Service arrives with half-a-dozen portions of waffles rather than just one!

Circle the portion that was meant for you – it's slightly different from the rest.

Answer on page 109

A.

B.

C.

D.

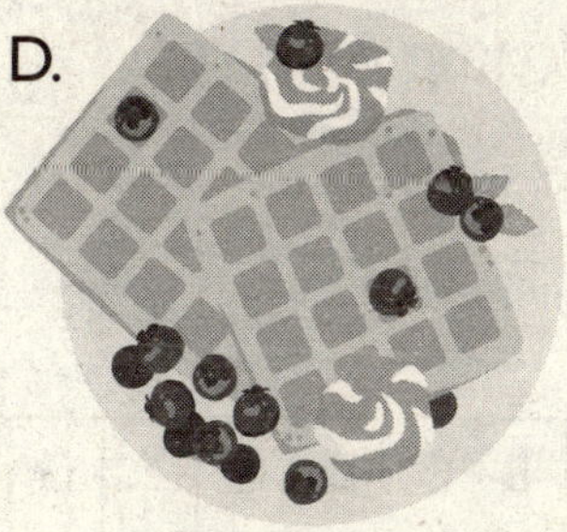

E.

F.

HARTIGAN'S HINT: The dish that belongs to you has a bonus blueberry!

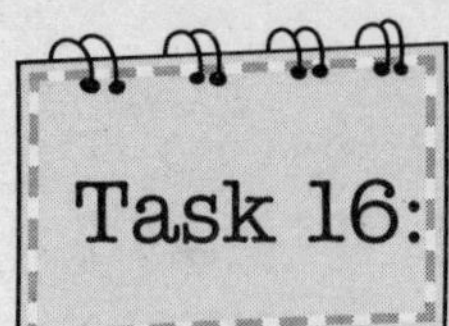

Task 16: Room Reservation

Your next case takes place on the picture-perfect archipelago of Zanzibar. A hotel room has been booked in your name at one of the following hotels, though I'll be a monkey's uncle if I can remember which!

Complete the key to decipher the names of the four fine hotels. Tick the box of the hotel that you think is expecting you.

Key:

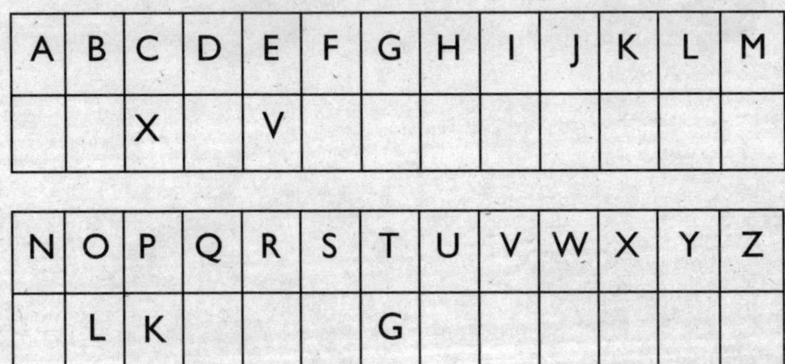

A	B	C	D	E	F	G	H	I	J	K	L	M
		X		V								

N	O	P	Q	R	S	T	U	V	W	X	Y	Z
	L	K			G							

HARTIGAN'S HINT: Someone's been monkeying around – this key is back to front!

1. The
KRMP UOZNRMTL

____ ________

2. The
IVW XLOLYFH

___ _______

3. The
YOZXP ISRML

_____ _____

4. The
HKLGGVW OVLKZIW

________ _______

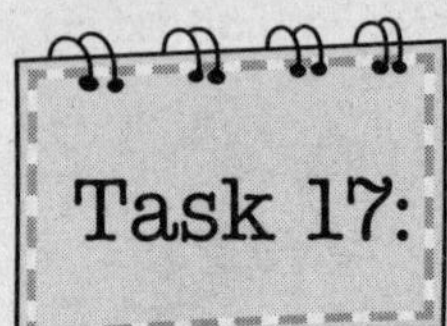

Task 17: A Dastardly Dazzle

While investigating suspicious wildlife tour, Safari So Good, you spot a gathering of stripy zebras . . . but all is not as it appears. Most are fibreglass fakes — installed to fool trusting tourists!

Only one of the dazzle is the real deal. Can you circle the true zebra?

HARTIGAN'S HINT: No two real zebras share the same stripes.

Answer on page 110

Task 18: The Venice Menace

Having tracked down the lock-up of local baddie Nic Da Lotte in Venice, you now need the code to the combination lock. Who knows what swag could be inside!

Nic is safely in police custody, but claims she can't remember the code. She did set a puzzle for herself in the event of sudden amnesia. Can you work it out?

Solve the number problems, then cross out the correct answers in the grid. Put the remaining numbers in order from smallest to largest to reveal the code.

A.   12 x 3   =

B.   100 – 50   =

C.   4 + 4   =

D.   12 ÷ 6   =

E.   11 x 4   =

F.   24 – 8   =

36	16	8
50	4	6
7	44	2

The code is:

Inside the lock-up, you discover a treasure trove of items, no doubt belonging to unwitting tourists. Handbags, wallets, phones and more! *Bravissimo*, detective!

Answer on page 111

Task 19: Left Luggage

Today's task requires you to collect a briefcase from the left luggage facilities at Paris's famous train station, Gare du Nord. You have the ticket to claim it, but are lacking the code to open the case.

To avoid the contents of the briefcase falling into enemy hands, its code has been encrypted using the Pigpen Cipher.

Use the key, then work out the numbers you need to unscramble the locks.

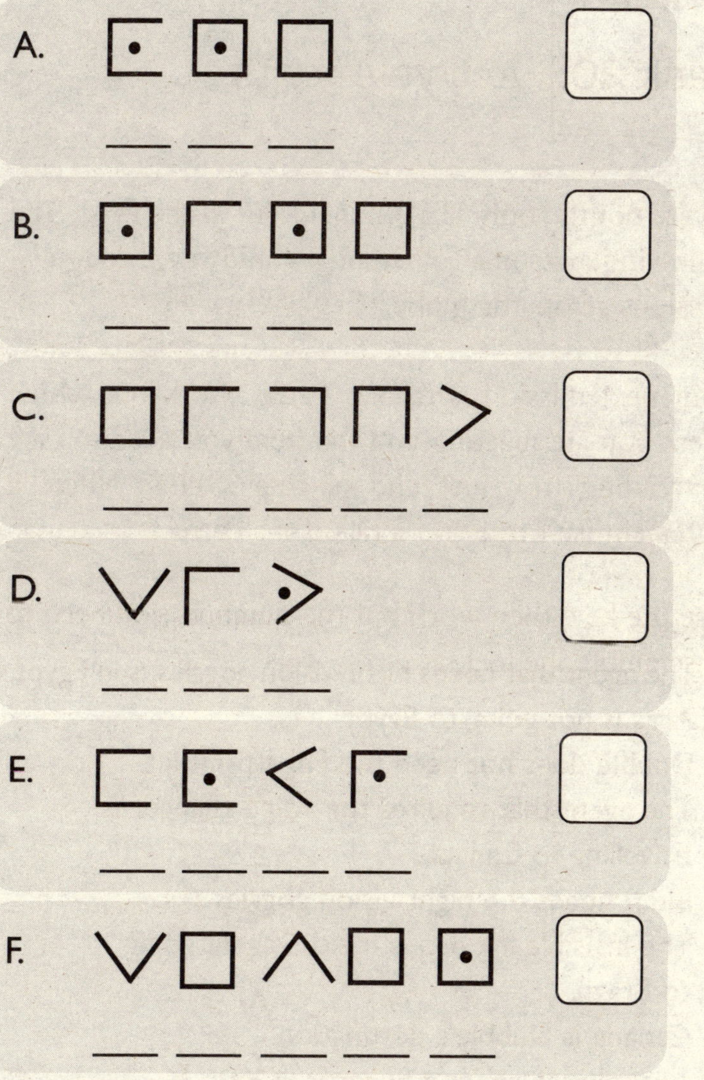

Hats off to you, or *chapeau*, I should I say! You'll find a croissant with your name on it at the station patisserie. Enjoy!

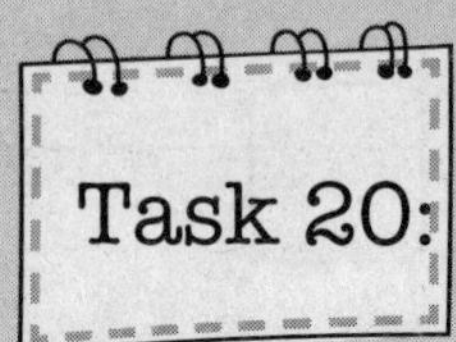

Task 20: Active Agents

You're not the only HBDA agent out in the field. The following awesome foursome are midway through missions across the globe.

Your next mission is to São Paulo. Work out which agent you are meeting and the item you need to take by reading the clues and placing a cross where a statement isn't true and a tick if it's correct.

Clues:
1. The agent that needs night-vision goggles is in Egypt.
2. Alias is not going to Egypt.
3. Dubble does not need the fingerprint kit.
4. The agent that requires the voice changer is travelling to Canada.
5. Blunt needs the night-vision goggles.
6. The invisible ink pen is for the agent going to Brazil.
7. Canada is Dubble's destination.
8. Alias always needs a fingerprint kit.

HARTIGAN'S HINT: Mark your answers in pencil, and keep an eraser hand to eliminate errors!

		Gadgets				Destinations			
		invisible ink pen	night-vision goggles	fingerprint kit	voice changer	Brazil	Egypt	Canada	Japan
Agents	Agent Alias								
	Inspector Blunt								
	P.I. Crouch								
	Detective Dubble								
Destinations	Brazil								
	Egypt								
	Canada								
	Japan								

You will be joining ________________________ in Brazil.

Remember to pack the ____________________ !

Answer on page 112

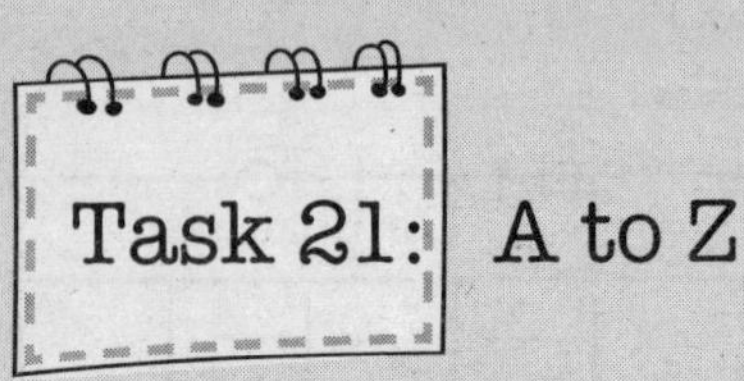

Task 21: A to Z

The phonetic alphabet has saved many a communication mishap since it was first introduced about a century ago. Standard code words are used to spell out words over the radio or in noisy environments, making messages quick and easy to understand. Here's the alphabet in full . . . study it carefully.

A = ALPHA	J = JULIET	S = SIERRA
B = BRAVO	K = KILO	T = TANGO
C = CHARLIE	L = LIMA	U = UNIFORM
D = DELTA	M = MIKE	V = VICTOR
E = ECHO	N = NOVEMBER	W = WHISKEY
F = FOXTROT	O = OSCAR	X = X-RAY
G = GOLF	P = PAPA	Y = YANKEE
H = HOTEL	Q = QUEBEC	Z = ZULU
I = INDIA	R = ROMEO	

So **AGENT** becomes

ALPHA-GOLF-ECHO-NOVEMBER-TANGO.

I'm about to share the names of five landmarks that belong to the same city in Europe – which is conveniently the destination for your next mission. What luck!

1. ALPHA-ROMEO-CHARLIE   DELTA-ECHO

__ __   __ __   __ __   __ __   __ __

TANGO-ROMEO-INDIA-OSCAR-MIKE-PAPA-HOTEL-ECHO

__ __   __ __   __ __   __ __   __ __

2. NOVEMBER-OSCAR-TANGO-ROMEO-ECHO

__ __   __ __   __ __   __ __   __ __

DELTA-ALPHA-MIKE-ECHO

__ __   __ __   __ __

3. LIMA-OSCAR-UNIFORM-VICTOR-ROMEO-ECHO

__ __   __ __   __ __   __ __   __ __   __ __

MIKE-UNIFORM-SIERRA-ECHO-UNIFORM-MIKE

__ __   __ __   __ __   __ __   __ __   __ __

4. ECHO-INDIA-FOXTROT-FOXTROT-ECHO-LIMA

__ __   __ __   __ __   __ __   __ __   __ __

TANGO-OSCAR-WHISKEY-ECHO-ROMEO

__ __   __ __   __ __   __ __

Your next mission is in: _______________________________

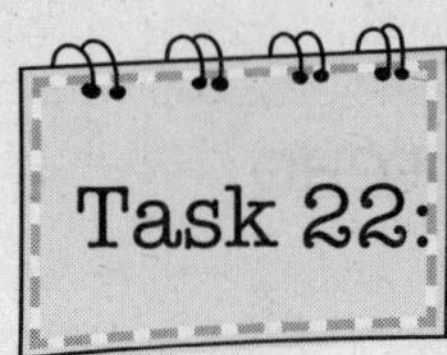

Task 22: Stowaway!

Unbeknown to its criminal crew, you've hitched a lift on board pirate ship the *Devil's Toenail* to keep a close eye on their plunderings.

A hidden message surrounds this ship's wheel with some sage advice for any passenger. Circle every second letter to reveal what it says.

Workings out:

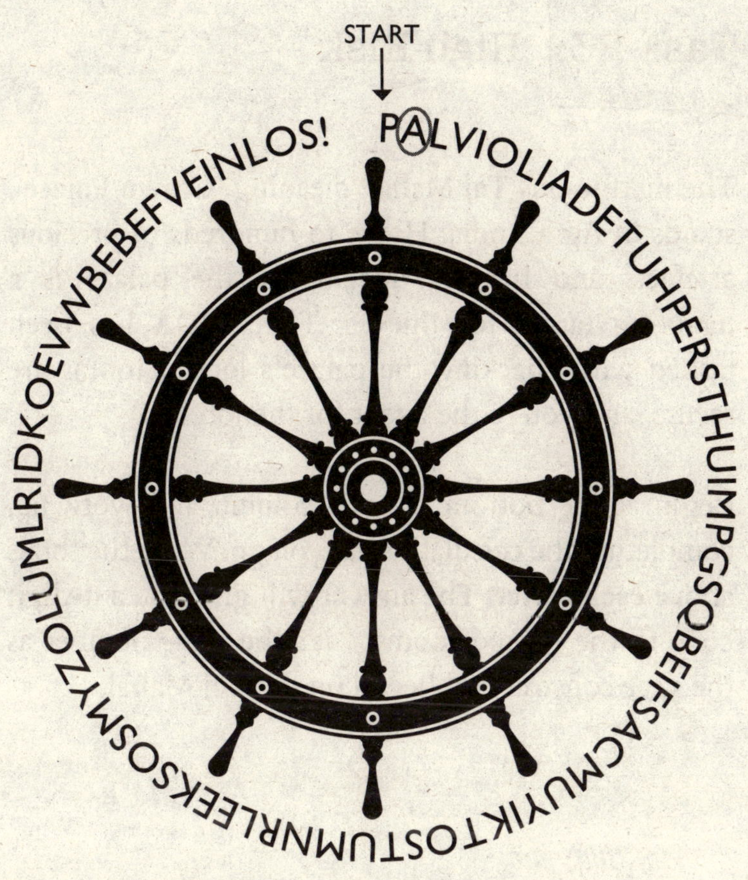

Write your answer here: _ _ _ _ _ _ _   _ _ _

_ _ _ _ ' _   _ _ _ _ _ _ _ _

_ _ _ _ _ _   _ _ _   _ _ _ _

_ _ _ _ _ _ _ _ !

Task 23: High Risk

The marble-ous Taj Mahal, meaning 'Crown Palace', stands in Agra, India. Home to hundreds of precious artefacts and historic documents, the palace is a tempting target for thieves. The HBDA has been tasked with checking the palace's locked rooms are secure, and you're the agent for the job.

Begin at the bottom of each column and work up, completing the calculations as you go. Write the totals above each tower. The answer will give you a 4-digit code to the locked rooms – it's the same number as the year construction began on the Taj Mahal.

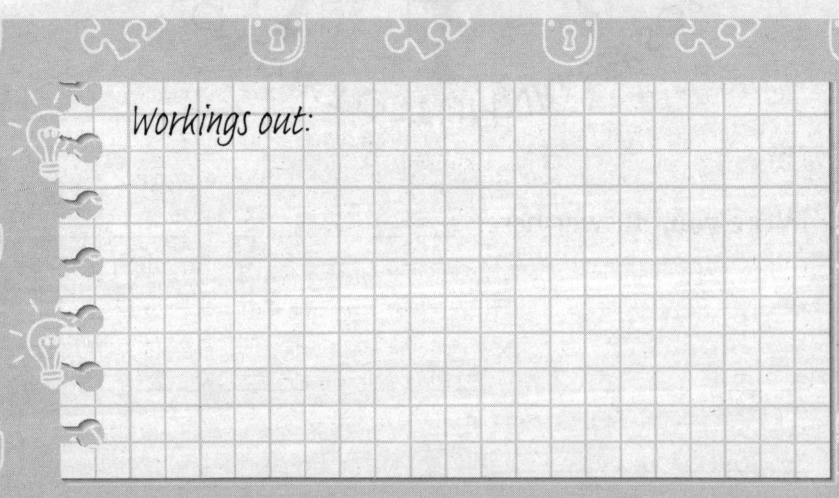

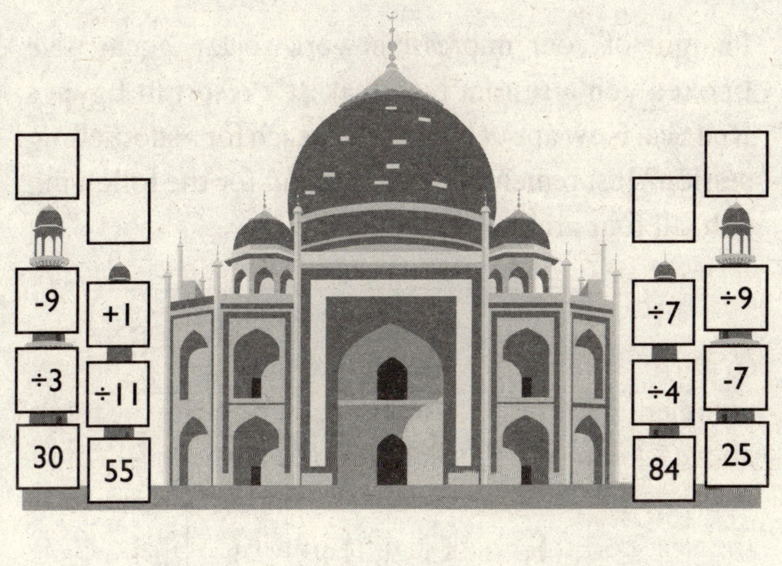

The code is:

I'm overjoyed to hear that everything is in order inside the palace, all thanks to your marvellous mathematical mind!

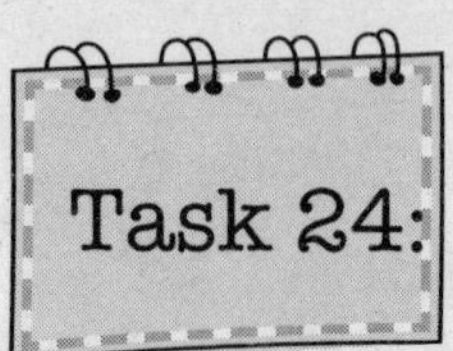

In light of your impressive work so far, agent, I've booked you a restorative break at a resort in Egypt's Red Sea. How about hitting the beach for a snorkelling session? Just remember to watch out for the following fish, all four are less than friendly!

	1	2	3	4	5
1	A	B	C	D	E
2	F	G	H	I	J
3	K	L	M	N	O
4	P	Q	R	S	T
5	U	V	W	X/Y	Z

Decode the numbers below to complete the names of the deadly fish. To find the right letters, first read along the grid, then go down.

A. 14, 15, 12, 12, 51, 34, 12, 42, 44, 32

_ _ _ _ _ _ _ _ _ _

B. 23, 42, 53, 43, 12, 42, 44, 32

_ _ _ _ _ _ _ _

C. 44, 54, 53, 43, 51, 12, 42, 44, 32

_ _ _ _ _ _ _ _ _

D. 44, 31, 53, 34, 14, 42, 53, 43, 12, 42, 44, 32

_ _ _ _ _ _ _ _ _ _ _ _

HARTIGAN'S HINT: To speed things up, take heed of how each clue ends.

Task 25: Flip-flopping

Following your refreshing Red Sea swim, you're faced with a slight problem back on dry land. Snorkelling, it seems, is a popular activity. Count how many pairs of flip-flops there are, then circle the pair that belongs to you.

HARTIGAN'S HINT: When it comes to footwear, you always stick to a simple style.

How many pairs of flip-flops are there?

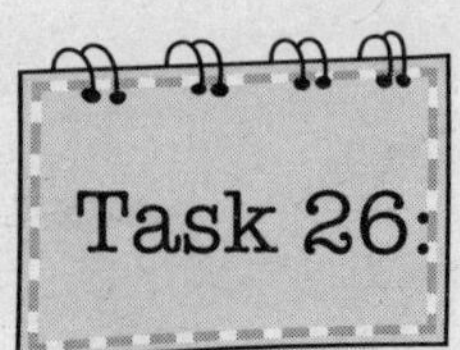

Task 26: Splashing Out

Filip van Dolphin is the prime suspect in the theft of a banana boat. Rumour has it, he's on his way to Splashing Out, a local water park, to try to offload the stolen goods.

You need to get to the water park quickly, detective! Pack your bag by placing the words below into the grid opposite. Place each word only once. Two letters have started you off.

Four Letters
KEYS

Five Letters
PHONE
TOWEL

Six Letters
SNACKS

Seven Letters
GOGGLES

Eight Letters
SWIMWEAR

Nine Letters
DISGUISES
SUNSCREEN

Ten Letters
SUNGLASSES
HEADPHONES

HARTIGAN'S HINT: Begin by placing words where there is only one option, counting the number of spaces in the grid.

Stand down, agent! It seems even criminals take a day off! Filip's just here to swim this time, but let's keep a watchful eye.

Answer on page 114

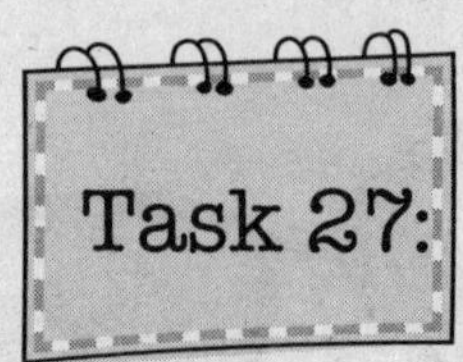 Task 27: Island Hopping

One backpacking baddie, a Mr Archie Pelago, is wanted for failing to pay for his lodgings at a number of island residences.

Your task is to track him down before he upsets more islanders with his moonlight flits. The clock is ticking!

Make your way from hut to hut in twenty or fewer moves, avoiding any broken bridges.

A bridge too far? Not likely! As a result of your nifty navigation, Archie is swiftly arrested and placed behind bars before bedtime.

Task 28: Opening Doors

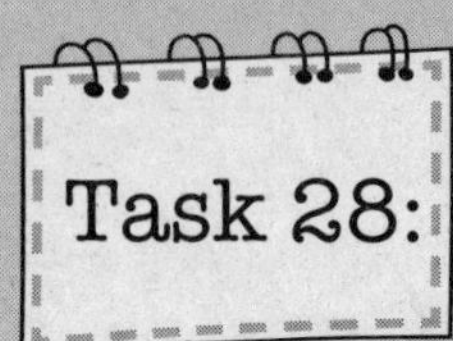

On your next stopover, Agent Tabitha Tan has offered you the use of her Singapore studio while she's engaged on a mission elsewhere. She's kindly said to help yourself to snacks!

The life of a globe-trotting agent is not without its trials, though: first you must find the correct key to gain entry to the studio. To find the correct key, read the clues below and cross the wrong keys out as you go. Circle the key for Tabitha's studio.

Clues:

The room number is:

- a 2-digit number
- an odd number
- a prime number
- the largest remaining number

Clever sausage! You're fast becoming a key player on my team. Now why not reward yourself with something tasty from the fridge?

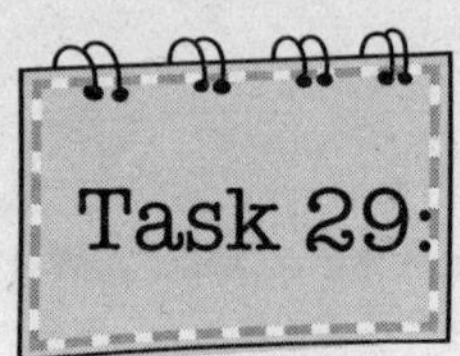

Task 29: Find the Fakes

A keen eye is needed in the ancient city of Athens. Can you identify the genuine treasures among these fakes? Each original is a one-off and looks different from the others.

First, circle the true treasure among these bogus busts.

Now try to spot the valid vase among the imitations.

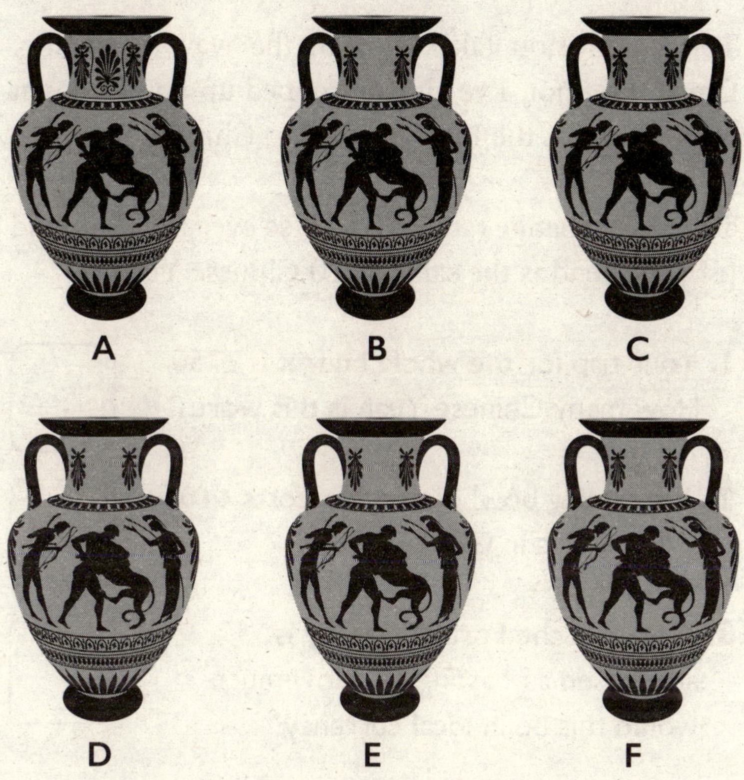

Task 30: Spending Money

Today's mission takes you all the way to Beijing, China. Fret not, I've already topped up your account with plenty of the local currency – Chinese Yuan.

Today's exchange rate is 10 to 1, so every 1 GB pound (£) you spend is the same as 10 Chinese Yuan (¥).

1. Your trip for the whole budget is £250. How many Chinese Yuan is this worth?

2. A steaming bowl of noodles costs ¥10. What is this in GBP?

3. A tour of the Forbidden City is advertised as costing £4. How much would this be in local currency?

4. A ticket on the subway back to the airport costs ¥30. What is this in GBP?

5. At the end of your trip, you are left with ¥60. How many GBP does this work out as?

A fairly frugal trip! Good job, as pricey Tokyo is the next stop on your Asian adventure!

It's time to get to grips with a new currency — the Japanese Yen. You land in Tokyo and learn that you'll get ¥200 for every £1. I've added more funds to your virtual wallet. Now try these sums:

6. You decide to exchange the British pounds you had left over from China. How much does this work out as in Japanese Yen?

7. A plate of sushi costs ¥3,000. What's that in GBP?

8. A trip up the Tokyo Tower comes in at £11. How much is a ticket in Yen?

9. You treat yourself to a new gadget. A mini spy camera costs ¥6,000. How much is this in GBP?

Good job, detective! You're a natural.

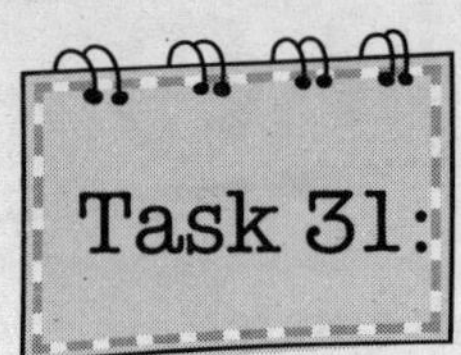

Task 31: Crack on to Krakow

Polish agent Gotfryd Goulash has recommended somewhere for a bite to eat on your latest mission, the cobbled city of Krakow.

To find out where you're meeting Goulash, decode the musical message using the key below.

Key:

Now use the key to work out the correct letters below each note to reveal the name of your lunchtime destination.

Location unlocked – that's music to my ears!

Twice the Vice

Detroit's Police Chief, Marshall Makepeace, has asked for your help because the police computer files are corrupt!

You soon work out the bug in the police files – the vowels in the names of five suspects have shifted to the next one along! Use the key to help you work out their real names.

Key:

Corrupted vowel:	Correct vowel:
E	A
I	E
O	I
U	O
A	U

1. OMMY T**ETI**

_MMY T_T_

2. H**E**NS **U**FF

H_NS _FF

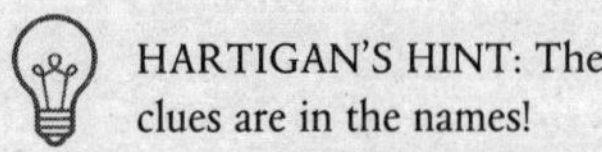

HARTIGAN'S HINT: The clues are in the names!

Now fill in the crime report below by matching the crime to the most likely suspect:

Crime:	Name of suspect:
bad graffiti	
pickpocketing	
identity theft	
breaking and entering	
getaway driver	

An awesome result, as our friends across the pond might say! With the suspects' names now confirmed, Chief Makepeace sends police cars to round up the motley mob.

Your services are next required at Egypt's Great Pyramid. Here comes the head-scratcher . . . raiders have actually returned treasure to Pharaoh Khufu's tomb, deep inside the pyramid! Spooked by a visit from the Pharaoh himself, perhaps? Oh, Mummy!

Make your way to the middle of the maze to check and photograph the treasure. Follow one rule – you must pass odd numbers only on your route.

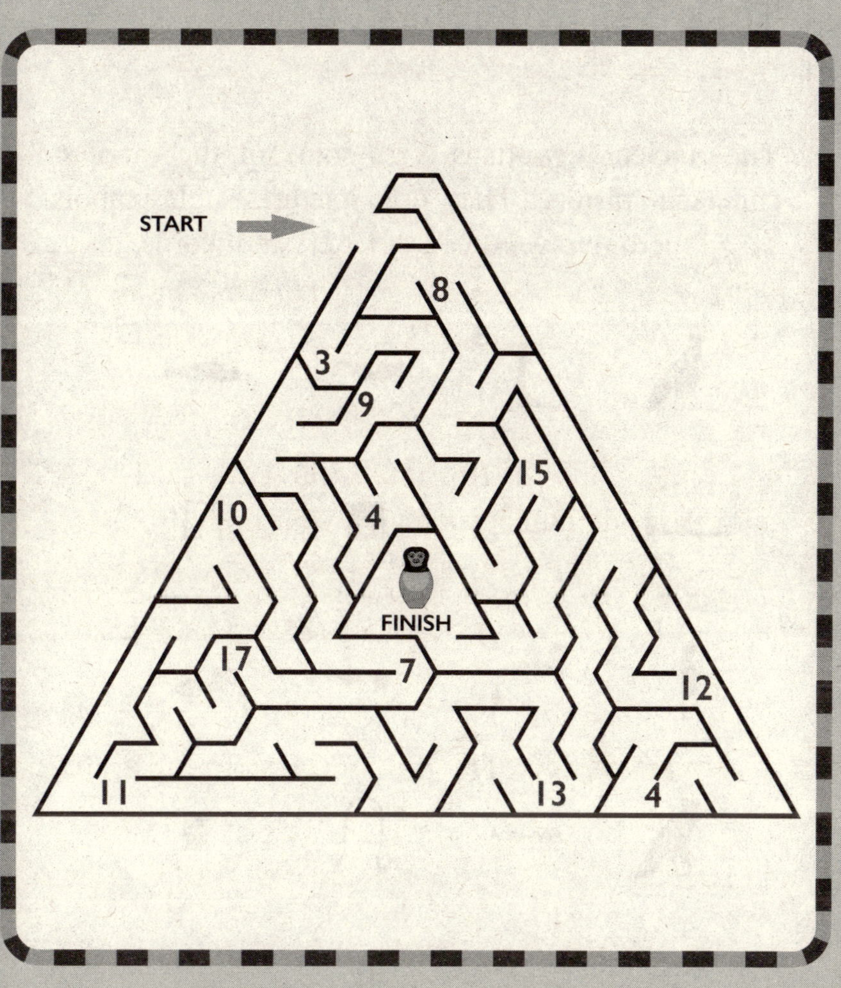

Pharaoh-nomenal detective work!

Task 34: Ancient Code

The Ancient Egyptians were some of the canniest coders in history! They used pictures and symbols called hieroglyphs instead of letters and words.

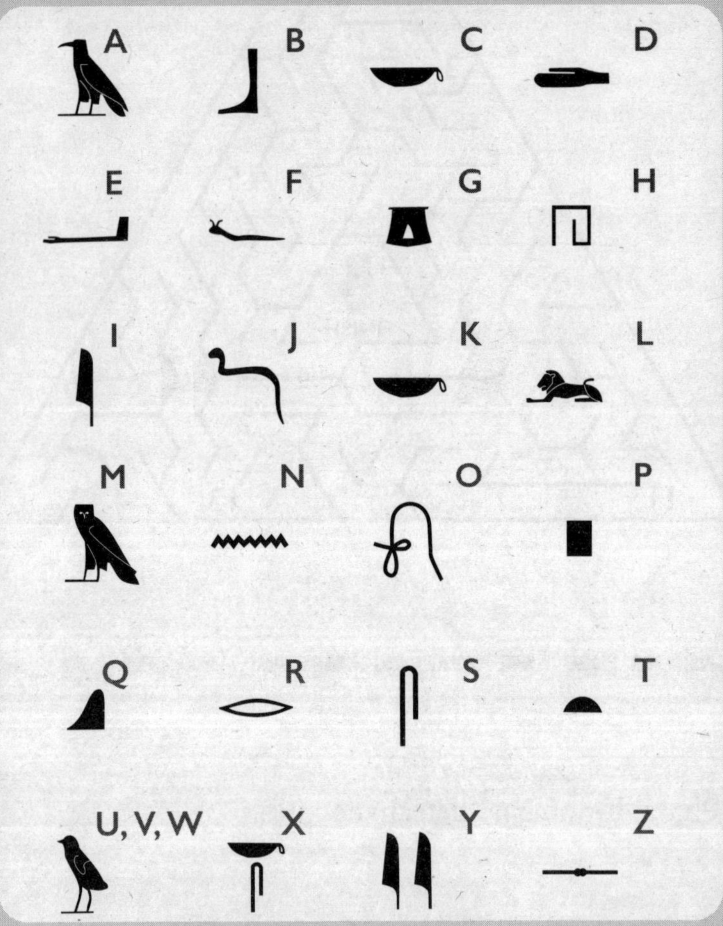

Use the hieroglyphic alphabet to work out the names
of the vessels that protected the organs of the deceased
for the afterlife. How delightful!

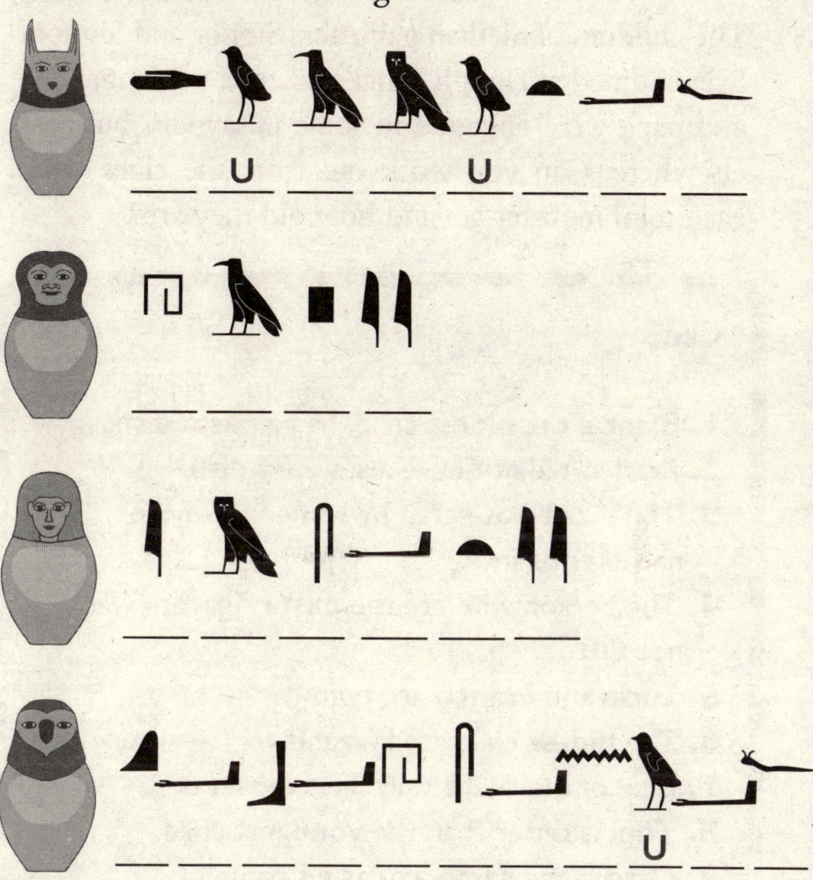

Which vessel did you discover in the Great Pyramid
of Giza (on page 67)?

____

Task 35: What a Mob!

The children of Sicilian gangsters Signor and Signora Salami dined at Dough Vinci's pizzeria while mamma and papa were engaged in some unsavoury business elsewhere. Can you work out from the clues what each mini mobster ate and how old they are?

Clues:

1. Bianca, the **oldest** child, had a **pasta dish**.
2. Franco did not have a **savoury dish**.
3. The **pizza** was eaten by someone whose name ends in A.
4. The person who ate the **pasta rigatoni** was not **Otto**.
5. Lucia and Franco are twins.
6. The **oldest** child ate **lasagne**.
7. One of the **twins** only likes **desserts**.
8. Toni is **older** than the **youngest** child.
9. Otto is the **same age** as his name!
10. Two of the children's names **appear in the** dishes they ate.

HARTIGAN'S HINT: Mark your answers in pencil, and keep an eraser handy to eliminate errors!

Complete the table with ticks and
crosses as you collect the evidence.

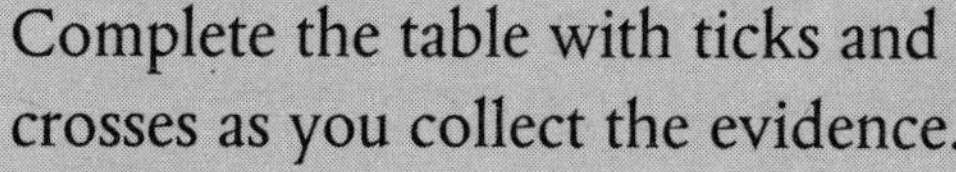

	Dishes					Ages			
	risotto	pasta rigatoni	lasagne	gelato	pizza	seven	eight	nine	ten
Children Otto									
Toni									
Blanca									
Franco									
Lucia									
Ages seven									
eight									
nine									
ten									

Which child do you think had the odd dish out?

____

Task 36: Good Times

I'm lending you a very special watch to take on the next leg of your journey, intrepid traveller, as African adventures await. You'll see that letters replace the usual numbers.

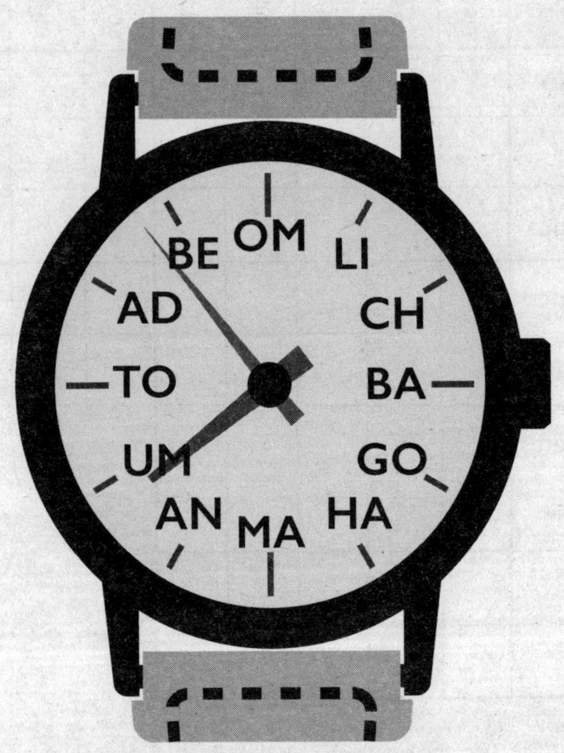

HARTIGAN'S HINT: The minute hand is the longer one!

First write the two letters shown by the minute hand, then the ones for the hour hand. Join them together to discover the names of three new nations on your itinerary and you're away!

1. Ten past ten ___ ___ ___ ___

2. Half past one ___ ___ ___ ___

3. Quarter to four ___ ___ ___ ___

Answer on page 119

Task 37: Mexican Menu

A Mexican fiesta at the Blue Cactus Cafe is on the cards next! First make your way through the maze, taking care to avoid any prickles.

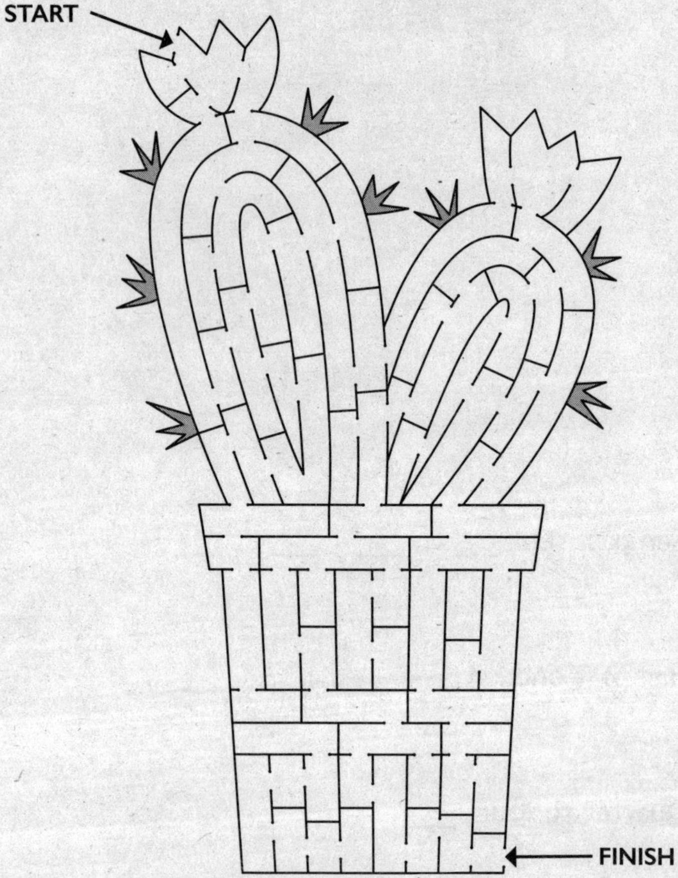

You arrive at the cafe to discover its menu is priced in a most peculiar way. Inspect it thoroughly, then work out how much they charge for nachos and churros.

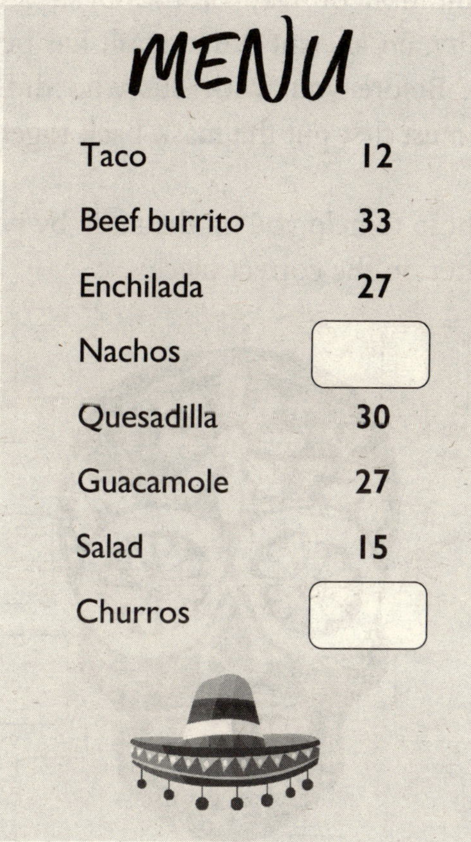

Bravo, detective! Now that's what I'm taco-ing about! *Ahem.*

 HARTIGAN'S HINT: Each letter has a value of three.

Task 38: Mask Task

At an exhibition of Day of the Dead artefacts in Mexico City, an ancient Aztec mask has been found destroyed. Before you work out who did this and why, you must first put the mask back together.

Use the photo to help you fix the mask by writing the correct letter on the correct piece.

How curious! One piece doesn't fit.

Which one is it? □

Splendid! You've fixed that in a jiffy! Now what's next, I wonder.

Answer on page 119

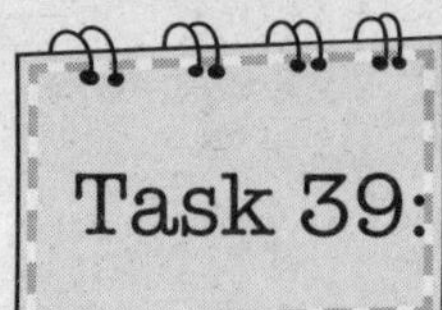

Task 39: Unburied Treasure

A treasure chest has been discovered by detective dog Digby on a beach. Give that plucky pup a treat! The treasure is thought to have belonged to a Captain Jet Blackbeard, who sailed the seas centuries ago.

The ancestors of Captain Blackbeard have kept in their possession three keys, cast in gold, silver and brass. One of the keys opens the lock, though they have no idea which.

Choose the correct key very carefully – the chest is believed to be boobytrapped!

Ready? Unscramble the clues, then circle the correct key.

_ _ _   _ _ _ _   _ _ _

_ _ _   _ _ _ _ _ _ _ _ _

_ _ _   _ _ _ _ _ _   _ _ _

HARTIGAN'S HINT: This is a golden opportunity to prove your detective skills!

Task 40: European Tour

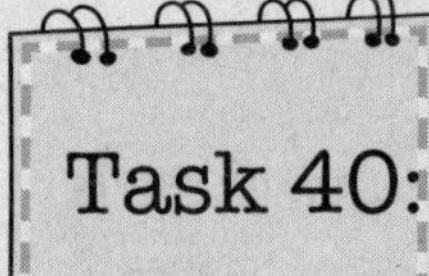

So far you've investigated suspects in eight countries across Europe. Fill in the missing letters from the country names to reveal where's next on your whistle-stop tour.

				O	L	A	N	D
	C	R		A	T	I	A	
		F		A	N	C	E	
	L	A		V	I	A		
		C		B	A			
B	U	L		A	R	I	A	
	S	P		I	N			
E	N	G		A	N	D		

HARTIGAN'S HINT: Complete the names of the countries you know first then return to any that prove a sterner test.

Well done, chum! Now to investigate some surly surfers accused of sea rage! Gnarly indeed. Starting at the letter A, drive through the grid in the order of the alphabet to reach the Atlantic coast at letter Z.

	A	R	G	H	I	J
	B	E	F	M	L	K
K	F	C	D	O	N	U	V
T	W	D	X	P	O	B	W
G	F	E	A	Q	X	Y	X
H	W	S	Z	R	W	Z	O
I	Y	M	N	S	V
J	K	L	U	T	U

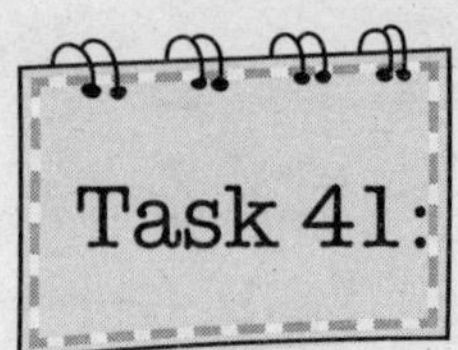

 Computer Genius

After a successful mission to Silicon Valley, you have come into the possession of equipment belonging to a group of expert hackers known as the Byte Brothers.

Computers rely on a secret language called binary code to understand information, which uses only two numbers: **0** and **1**. Prove your genius by filling in the blanks on each computer screen to complete the binary code puzzles.

Rules:

1. Each box should contain either a zero or a one.
2. More than two equal numbers immediately next to or below each other are not allowed.
3. Each row and each column should contain an equal number of zeros and ones.
4. Each row is unique and each column is unique – any row cannot be exactly equal to another row, and any column cannot be exactly equal to another column.

Easy:

		0	
1	1	0	
		1	1
0			0

Harder:

	0		0
0		1	
0	1		

Even harder:

0	0				1
0				0	
1	1	0	0	1	
		0	0		1
1					0
	1		1	0	0

Answer on page 121

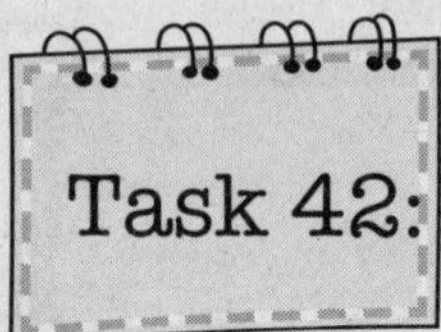

A Vanished Vessel

Your next case is across the Atlantic Ocean, to look into the disappearance of a fishing vessel that has vanished without a trace.

Our Caribbean correspondent San Juan has sent you a message with the last known location of the ship. Let's see if you can work it out . . .

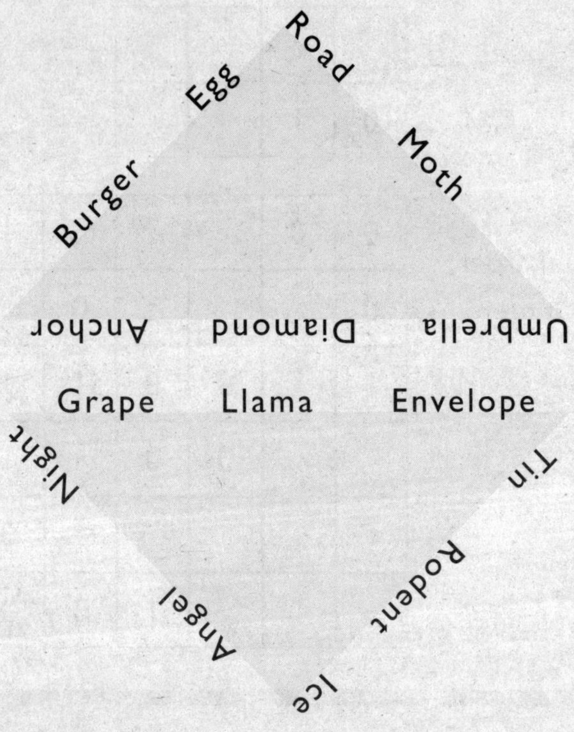

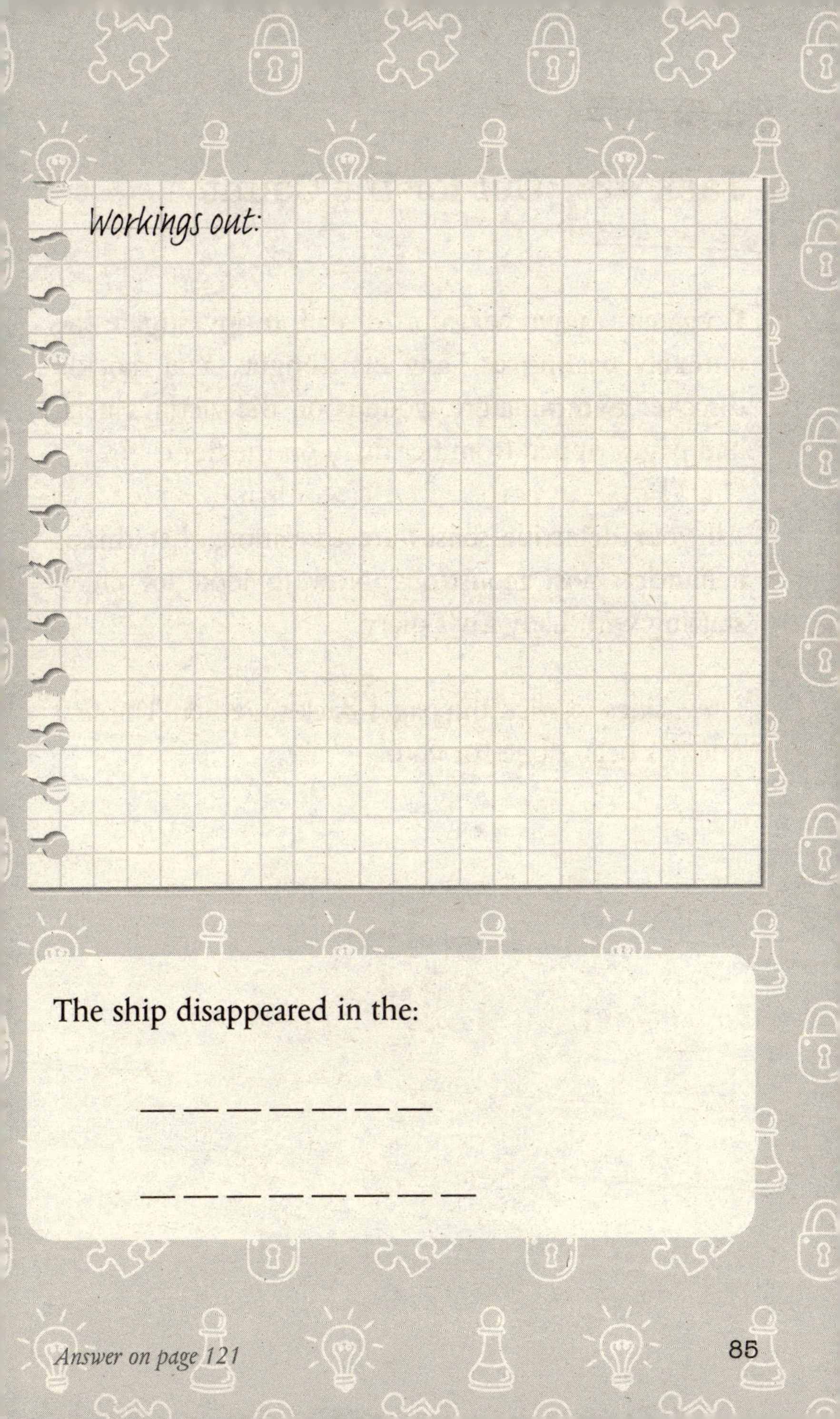

The ship disappeared in the:

_ _ _ _ _ _ _

_ _ _ _ _ _ _ _

Task 43: Out for the Count

Romania is your next port of call, to investigate the untimely passing of Lady Liv Longue. You quickly discover two puncture wounds on the victim's neck and pages ripped from her diary on the floor.

All your detective senses are screaming that this is a murder most monstrous! Now to look for clues, starting with Lady Liv's diary.

Draw lines to stick the pages back together. The first one has been done for you.

The name of a creepy count appears in multiple entries of Lady Longue's diary. You pass on the name to police, then make a sharp exit.

Answer on page 121

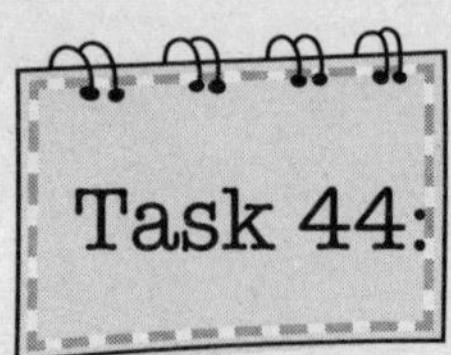

Task 44: Sheikh a Leg

You've trekked to Morocco's Sahara Desert, to observe a fake sheikh and his faithful getaway camel. The sheikh can't resist showing off his cameline chum's speed and has entered a race.

We know that the sheikh's camel is far faster than the average ship of the desert. Find the quickest camel by adding the next number in each sequence.

A. Humphrey

11   22   33   44   km/h

B. Camela

4   8   16   32   km/h

C. June

95   85   75   65   km/h

D. Dusty

18   27   36   45   km/h

The quickest camel is ______________________

with a top speed of ________________ km/h.

Wait a minute, that camel is the spit of one that went missing from Morocco's national zoo! You call the zoo to rescue their resident while the police take the fake sheikh into custody.

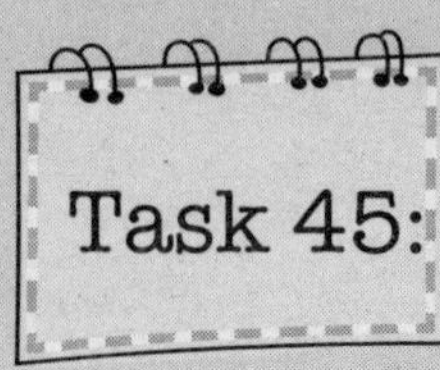

Task 45: Off Her Trolley

Well this is a turn up for the books! The light-fingered Miss De Meanour has seen the error of her ways and returned a host of stolen items to the store.

Circle eight things that have changed in the supermarket scene below.

Task 46: Half the Story

A memo from Floridian agent Flora Fleet is waiting for you at the desk of the Motel California, though it appears only 50 per cent of it has been scribbled down. Work out what Fleet is trying to tell you by drawing the mirror images to complete the words and numbers.

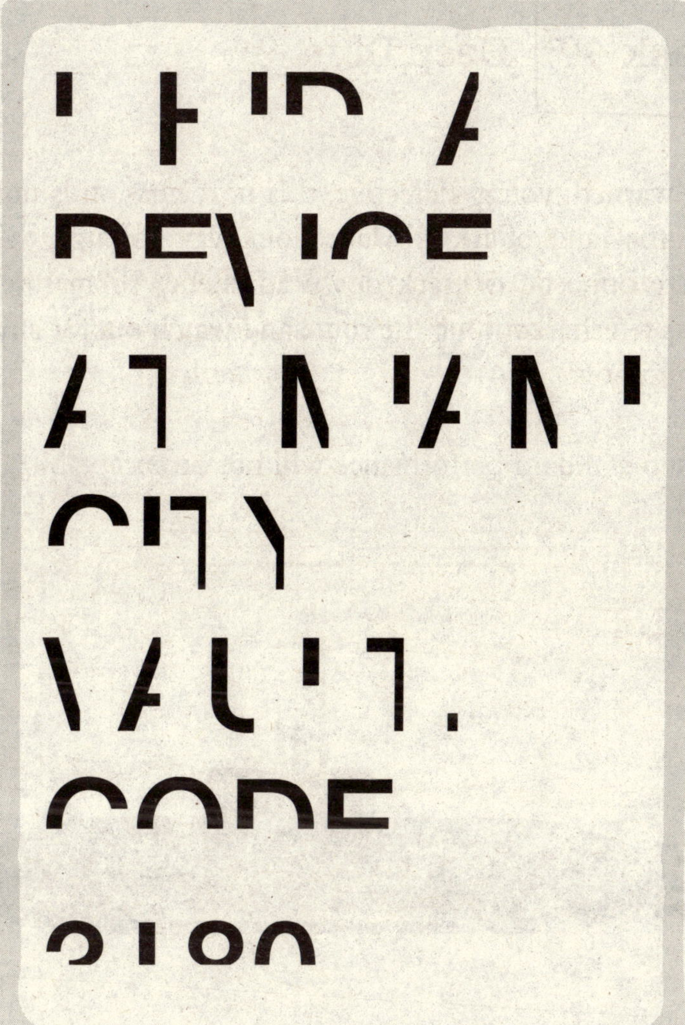

Hurrah! You made light work of that memo! Now make haste to retrieve Fleet's package.

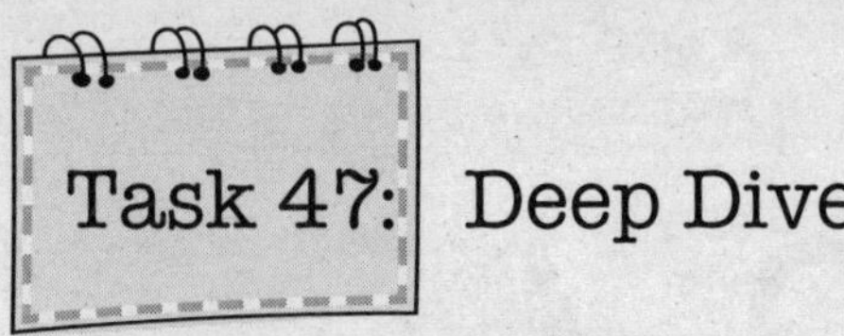

Be warned, young detective, this next mission is not for the faint of heart. Make your way through the maze opposite to track down an enemy submarine. Pass ten sharks along the route and watch out for any whirlpools.

A sub-standard performance will not be acceptable!

Shipshape! Those sharks and whirlpools didn't slow you down for a second!

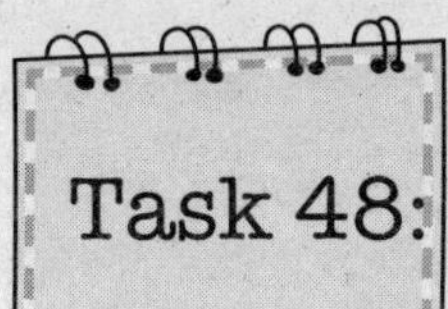

Task 48: City Slicker

A hop across the pond is where your detective work takes you next. Try to snooze on the flight over, as you won't sleep much during your stay in this city!

Crack the code to find out the names of four famous landmarks and reveal your destination.

Key

	1	2	3	4	5
1	A	B	C	D	E
2	F	G	H	I	J
3	K	L	M	N	O
4	P	Q	R	S	T
5	U	V	W	X/Y	Z

Example: 41, 53, 22 would make the word DOG.

HARTIGAN'S HINT: Move horizontally along the row to find the first digit, then vertically for the second.

A. 54, 42, 33, 51, 44   44, 24, 15, 11, 34, 51

_ _ _ _ _ _ _ _ _ _ _

B. 51, 33, 14, 42, 34, 51   44, 54, 11, 54, 51

_ _ _ _ _ _ _ _ _ _ _

21, 15, 42, 23, 41, 42, 43, 22

_ _ _ _ _ _ _ _

C. 44, 54, 11, 54, 15, 51   53, 12

_ _ _ _ _ _ _ _ _ _

23, 42, 21, 51, 34, 54, 45

_ _ _ _ _ _ _

D. 31, 51, 43, 54, 34, 11, 23 14, 11, 34, 13

_ _ _ _ _ _ _ _ _ _ _

The city is: _______________________________

Task 49: Tardy Twins

Canadian car thieves the Tailpipe Twins have met every day this week so far, but the time they meet gets later and later each day. Study the times of their rendezvous, then predict what time they will meet on Thursday and Friday.

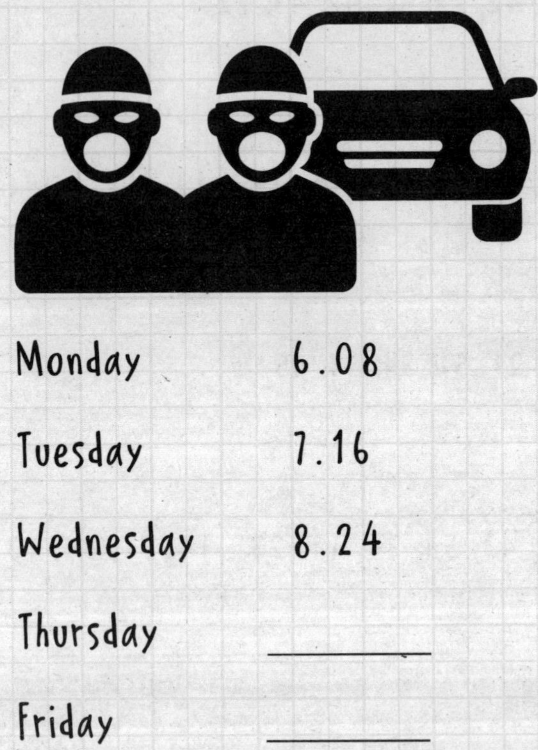

Monday	6.08
Tuesday	7.16
Wednesday	8.24
Thursday	_______
Friday	_______

HARTIGAN'S HINT: Stumped on the second part of the task? I find flipping the puzzle on its head often helps!

The twins have plans to steal another desirable motor from priority parking at Prince George Airport. Can you work out the number of the space in which the car is parked?

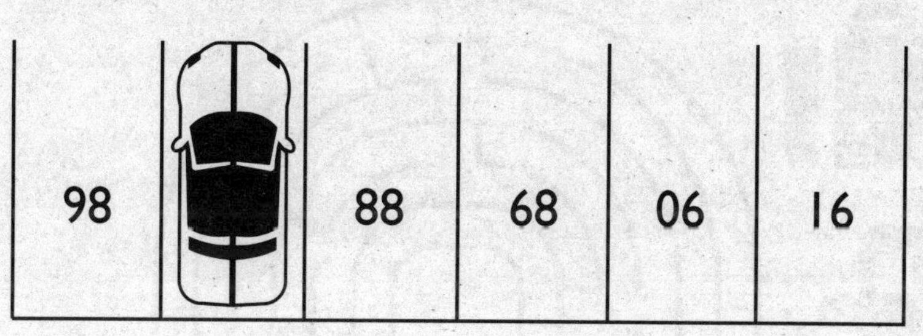

Answer:

Bravo, detective! You're really motoring now.

Task 50: Carousel Ride

Hurrah, your final flight has landed safe and sound! One last task awaits before you can go off-duty. Draw a path to guide this luggage along the baggage carousel, then collect your case.

Answer on page 124

Congratulazioni! ¡Felicidades! Bravo, young detective! You've cracked dozens of cases across the globe – from the Americas to Asia, Europe, Africa and Australia!

It is my honour to bestow upon you a new Hartigan Browne Detective Agency badge that befits your epic adventure! Flash this at passport control in any country and you'll sail right on through.

Agent

NAME:___________________________

ANSWERS

Task 1: What Am I?

From page 2

1. STAMP
2. ANCHOR
3. FOOTSTEPS

Task 2: Prepare for Take-off

From page 4

Answer is
PILOT

Task 3: Agents Abroad

From page 6

1. PUNCTUALITY
2. SENSE OF ADVENTURE
3. SEA LEGS
4. HEAD FOR HEIGHTS
5. CURIOSITY
6. LANGUAGE SKILLS
7. PHYSICAL FITNESS
8. SENSE OF DIRECTION

Task 4: Taking Flight

From page 8

Flight ZA302 to ZANZIBAR.

Task 5: Onwards and Upwards

From page 10

An unsolved crime is a COLD CASE.

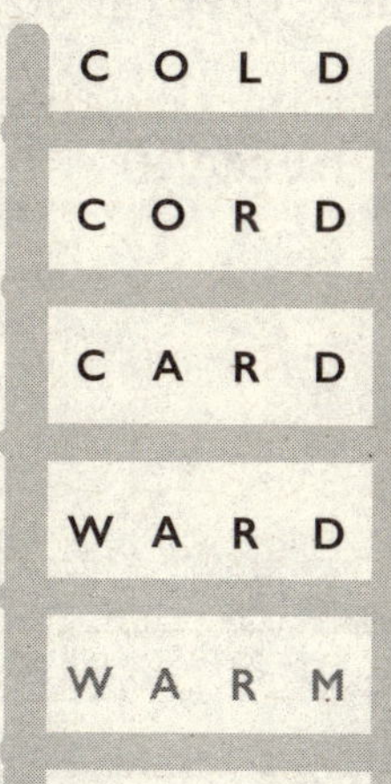

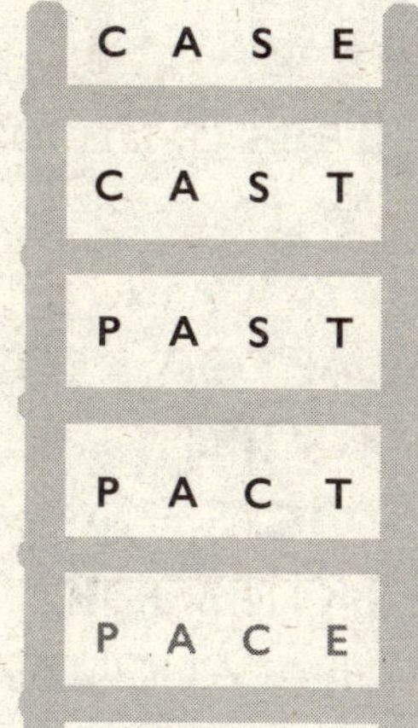

Task 6: New Connections
From page 12

A. Password: 1 3 4 7   **B.** Password: 2 4 6 8

<table>
<tr><td>8</td><td>1</td><td>6</td></tr>
<tr><td>3</td><td>5</td><td>7</td></tr>
<tr><td>4</td><td>9</td><td>2</td></tr>
</table>

<table>
<tr><td>2</td><td>7</td><td>6</td></tr>
<tr><td>9</td><td>5</td><td>1</td></tr>
<tr><td>4</td><td>3</td><td>8</td></tr>
</table>

Task 7: Port of Call
From page 14

The name of the boat is: KNOT SO FAST.
It is due to land in: PIER TWO at SIX O'CLOCK.

Task 8: Snoozing in Style
From page 16

LAP**T**OP
T-SH**I**RT
SO**C**KS
NOTEBOO**K**
HEADPHON**E**S
TOOTHBRUSH   The answer is: TICKET.

Task 9: Message in a Bottle

From page 18

REPORTED SIGHTINGS OF A MARINE MONSTER
AT THE LOCH. TAKE EXTRA CARE!

Task 10: Checking In

From page 20

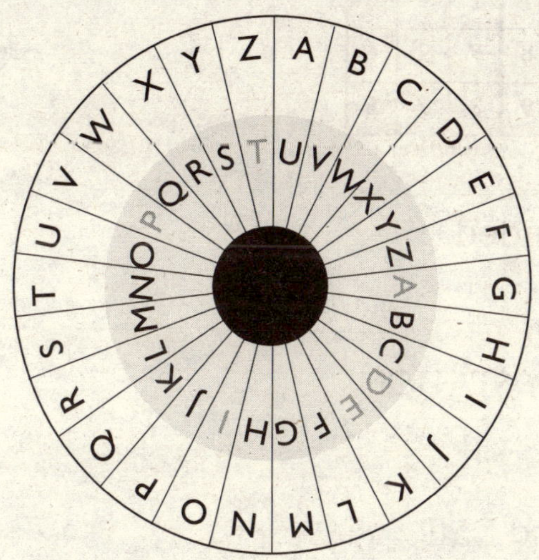

The message says: SOS! SEND A CHOPPER
TO VATICAN CITY HELIPAD, OPERATION
COMPROMISED!

Task 11: Out of Order

From page 22

2	3	4	9	5	6	8	1	7
9	5	7	8	1	4	2	6	3
1	8	6	3	7	2	4	5	9
5	4	9	6	8	1	7	3	2
6	1	8	7	2	3	5	9	4
7	2	3	4	9	5	6	8	1
3	9	2	5	6	7	1	4	8
4	7	5	1	3	8	9	2	6
8	6	1	2	4	9	3	7	5

The code is: 7145.

Task 12: Grounded

From page 24

GRAND SUBWAY STATION.

Task 13: Missed Call

From page 26

DEAD DROP. STEPS OF SOUTH TOWER.
TOWER BRIDGE.

Task 14: Take the Wheel

From page 28

1. SCOOTER
2. BICYCLE
3. AEROPLANE
4. MOTORBIKE

Task 15: Breakfast in Bed

From page 30

C.

Task 16: Room Reservation

From page 32

1. THE PINK FLAMINGO
2. THE RED COLOBUS
3. THE BLACK RHINO
4. THE SPOTTED LEOPARD

You'll be a distinguished guest at THE RED COLOBUS – the word 'monkey' in my instructions and hint was a clue!

Task 17: A Dastardly Dazzle

From page 34

Task 18: The Venice Menace

From page 36

A. 12 x 3 = 36
B. 100 – 50 = 50
C. 4 + 4 = 8
D. 12 ÷ 6 = 2
E. 11 x 4 = 44
F. 24 – 8 = 16

The code is: 467

Task 19: Left Luggage

From page 38

A. ONE   **C.** EIGHT   **E.** FOUR
B. NINE   **D.** SIX   **F.** SEVEN

Task 20: Active Agents

From page 40

You should expect to meet P.I. Crouch in São Paulo, Brazil with the invisible ink pen.

		Gadgets				Destinations			
		invisible ink pen	night-vision goggles	fingerprint kit	voice changer	Brazil	Egypt	Canada	Japan
Agents	Agent Alias	✗	✗	✓	✗	✗	✗	✗	✓
	Inspector Blunt	✗	✓	✗	✗	✗	✓	✗	✗
	P.I. Crouch	✓	✗	✗	✗	✓	✗	✗	✗
	Detective Dubble	✗	✗	✗	✓	✗	✗	✓	✗
Destinations	Brazil	✓	✗	✗	✗				
	Egypt	✗	✓	✗	✗				
	Canada	✗	✗	✗	✓				
	Japan	✗	✗	✓	✗				

Task 21: A to Z

From page 42

1. ARC DE TRIOMPHE
2. NOTRE-DAME
3. LOUVRE MUSEUM
4. EIFFEL TOWER

The city is: PARIS.

Task 22: Stowaway!
From page 44

AVOID THE SHIP'S BISCUITS UNLESS YOU LIKE WEEVILS!

Task 23: High Risk
From page 46

The code is 1632.

Task 24: Grim Swim

From page 48

A. PUFFERFISH   **C.** STONEFISH
B. LIONFISH   **D.** SCORPIONFISH

Task 25: Flip-flopping

From page 50

There are 13 pairs of flip-flops.
Yours are these ones:

Task 26:
Splashing Out

From page 52

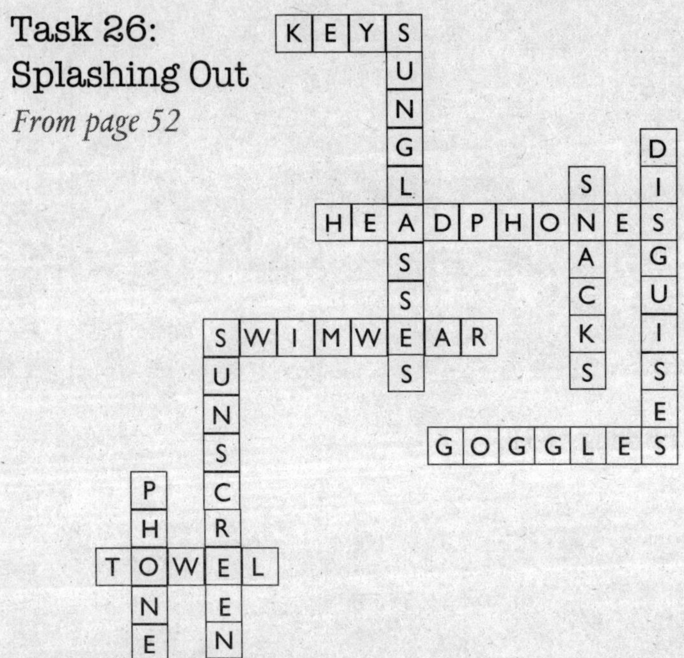

Task 27: Island Hopping

From page 54

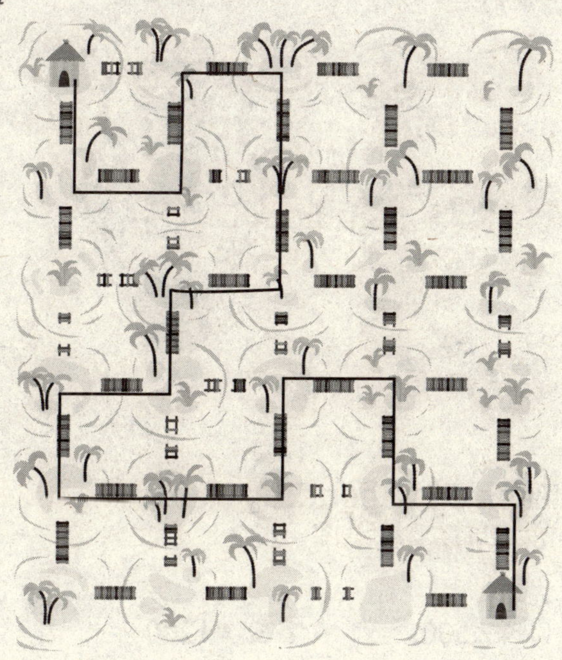

Task 28: Opening Doors

From page 56

Task 29: Find the Flakes
From page 58

E

A

Task 30: Spending Money
From page 60

1. ¥2,500
2. £1
3. ¥40
4. £3
5. £6
6. ¥1200
7. £15
8. ¥2200
9. £30

Task 31: Crack on to Krakow
From page 62

CABBAGE CAFE

Task 32: Twice the Vice

From page 64

Crime:	Name of suspect:
bad graffiti	TAG VAN DAL
pickpocketing	HANS OFF
identity theft	IMMY TATE
breaking and entering	BUSTER LOCK
getaway driver	MILES O'SMOKE

Task 33: Giza Clue

From page 66

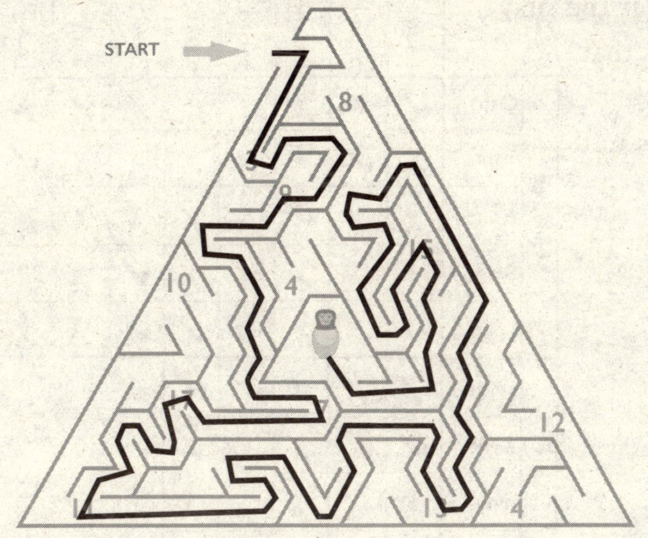

Task 34: Ancient Code

From page 68

1. DUAMUTEF
2. HAPY
3. IMSETY
4. QEBEHSENUEF

HAPY was the treasure in the Great Pyramid of Giza.

Task 35: What a Mob!

From page 70

Franco had the odd dish out — it was the only dish that was sweet.

		Dishes					Ages			
		risotto	pasta rigatoni	lasagne	gelato	pizza	seven	eight	nine	ten
Children	Otto	✔	✗	✗	✗	✗	✗	✔	✗	✗
	Toni	✗	✔	✗	✗	✗	✗	✗	✔	✗
	Bianca	✗	✗	✔	✗	✗	✗	✗	✗	✔
	Franco	✗	✗	✗	✔	✗	✔	✗	✗	✗
	Lucia	✗	✗	✗	✗	✔	✔	✗	✗	✗
Ages	seven	✗	✗	✗	✔	✔				
	eight	✔	✗	✗	✗	✗				
	nine	✗	✔	✗	✗	✗				
	ten	✗	✗	✔	✗	✗				

Task 36: Good Times

From page 72

1. CHAD   **2.** MALI   **3.** TOGO

Task 37: Mexican Menu

From page 74

Each letter has a value of 3.

Taco	12	Quesadilla	30
Beef burrito	33	Guacamole	27
Enchilada	27	Salad	15
Nachos	**18**	Churros	**21**

Task 38: Mask Task

From page 76

Piece D does not fit.

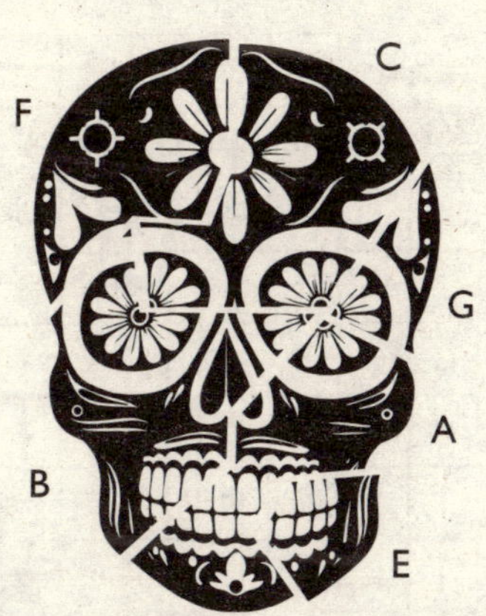

Task 39: Unburied Treasure

From page 78

1. EDENHGTYOKEL: THE GOLDEN KEY
2. RIVETSHYELKE: THE SILVER KEY
3. BYTESHAKERS: THE BRASS KEY

Task 40: European Tour

From page 80

The answer is:
PORTUGAL

			P	O	L	A	N	D
	C	R	O	A	T	I	A	
		F	R	A	N	C	E	
	L	A	T	V	I	A		
		C	U	B	A			
B	U	L	G	A	R	I	A	
	S	P	A	I	N			
E	N	G	L	A	N	D		

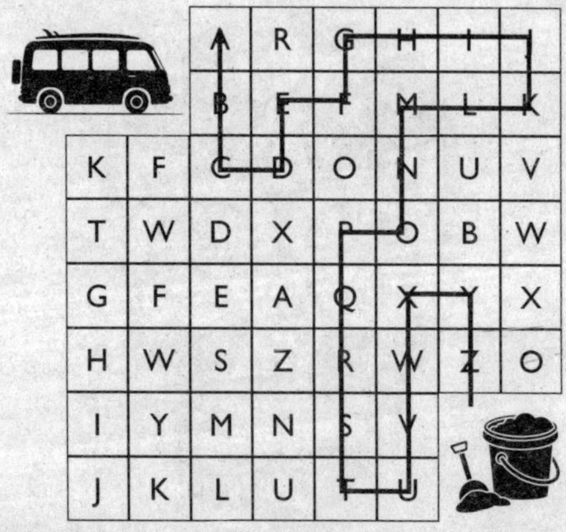

Task 41: Computer Genius

From page 82

1	0	0	1
1	1	0	0
0	0	1	1
0	1	1	0

1	0	1	0
0	1	1	0
1	0	0	1
0	1	0	1

0	0	1	0	1	1
0	0	1	1	0	1
1	1	0	0	1	0
0	1	0	0	1	1
1	0	1	1	0	0
1	1	0	1	0	0

Task 42: A Vanished Vessel

From page 84

The answer is: BERMUDA TRIANGLE, found by reading the initial letter of each word.

Task 43: Out for the Count

From page 86

1 → C   4 → A

2 → E   5 → D

3 → F   6 → B

Task 44: Sheikh a Leg

From page 88

A. Humphrey = 55 km/h
B. Camela = 64 km/h
C. Dune = 55 km/h
D. Dusty = 54 km/h

The fastest camel is Camela, with a top speed of 64 km/h.

Task 45: Off Her Trolley

From page 90

Task 46: Half the Story

From page 92

I HID A DEVICE AT MIAMI CITY VAULT. CODE 3180.

Task 47: Deep Dive

From page 94

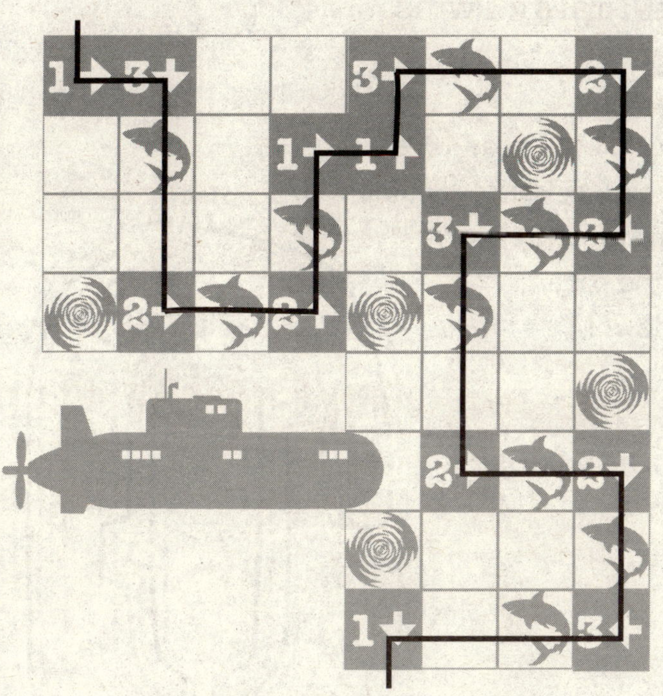

Task 48: City Slicker

From page 96

A. TIMES SQUARE   **C.** STATUE OF LIBERTY
B. EMPIRE STATE BUILDING **D.** CENTRAL PARK

The city is New York.

Task 49: Tardy Twins

From page 96

Thursday 9:32 / Friday 10.40
The car parking space is number 87.
You work it out by
turning the page
upside down!

Task 50: Carousel Ride

From page 100

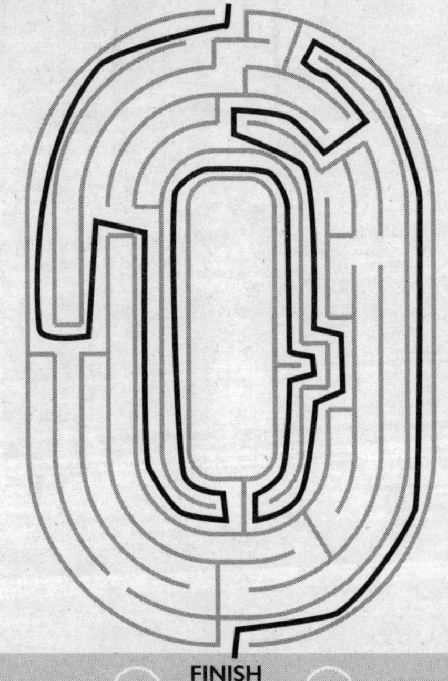